BEAUTIFUL OUTLAW

BEAUTIFUL OUTLAW

EXPERIENCING THE PLAYFUL, DISRUPTIVE, EXTRAVAGANT PERSONALITY OF JESUS

JOHN ELDREDGE

NEW YORK • BOSTON • NASHVILLE

(The Author) is represented by Yates & Yates, www.yates2.com.

Published in association with Yates & Yates, LLP, www.yates2.com.

Unless otherwise noted, Scripture quotations are from the Holy Bible, New International Version®. Copyright © 1973, 1978, 1984 by International Bible Society. Used by permission of Zondervan Publishing House. All rights reserved.
Scripture quotations noted NASB are from the New American Standard Bible®. Copyright © 1960, 1962, 1963, 1968, 1971, 1972, 1973, 1975, 1977, 1995 by The Lockman Foundation. Used by permission.
Scripture quotations noted NLT are from the *Holy Bible*, New Living Translation, copyright © 1996, 2004. Used by permission of Tyndale House Publishers, Inc., Wheaton, Illinois 60189. All rights reserved.
Scripture quotations noted NRSV are from the New Revised Standard Version of the Bible. Copyright © 1989 by the Division of Christian Education of the National Council of the Churches of Christ in the U.S.A. All rights reserved.
Scripture quotations noted The Message are taken from *The Message*. Copyright © 1993, 1994, 1995, 1996, 2000, 2001, 2002. Used by permission of NavPress Publishing Group.

FaithWords
Hachette Book Group
237 Park Avenue
New York, NY 10017

www.faithwords.com
Printed in the United States of America

First Edition: October 2011
10 9 8 7 6 5 4 3 2 1

FaithWords is a division of Hachette Book Group, Inc.
The FaithWords name and logo are trademarks of Hachette Book Group, Inc.

The publisher is not responsible for websites (or their content) that are not owned by the publisher.

Library of Congress Cataloging-in-Publication Data

Eldredge, John, 1960-
    Beautiful outlaw : experiencing the playful, disruptive, extravagant personality of Jesus / John Eldredge.—1st ed.
        p. cm.
    ISBN 978-0-89296-088-0 (regular edition)—ISBN 978-1-4555-0730-6 (large print edition)   1. Jesus Christ—Character.   2. Christian life.   I. Title.
    BT304.E34 2011
    232.9'03—dc23
                                        2011018090

The infinite Life of God himself took shape before us. We saw it, we heard it, and now we're telling you so you can experience it along with us, this experience of communion with the Father and his Son, Jesus Christ. Our motive for writing is simply this: We want you to enjoy this, too. (1 John 1:2–4 The Message)

CONTENTS

THE TIPPING OF THE LANDSLIDE

Sunlight on water.
Songbirds in a forest.
Desert sands under moonlight.
Vineyards just before harvest.

These all share something in common—they reflect the heart of a particular artist. They are his masterpieces, his expression and his gift to us. The artist's name is Jesus. Something else lies in common between these treasures and Jesus as well—words on a page cannot compare to a personal experience. Sailing the ocean on a bright morning with the wind in your face, wandering under a forest canopy while sunlight filters down, lying on warm dunes beneath a full moon watching shooting stars, drinking in the lush beauty of vineyards on a hillside in early autumn—these experiences are far closer to what it is actually like to experience Jesus than mere talk of him could ever be.

More words about Jesus are helpful *only* if they bring us to an experience of him.

We don't need further speculation or debate. We need Jesus himself. And you can have him. Really. You can experience Jesus intimately. You were meant to. For despite the vandalizing of Jesus Christ by religion and the world, he is still alive and very much himself. Though nowadays it takes a bit of uncovering to know him as he is. A simple prayer, at the outset, will loose encounters like a landslide:

Jesus, I ask you for you. For the real you.

For to have Jesus, really have him, is to have the greatest treasure in all worlds.

And to *love* Jesus—that is to settle the first question of human existence. Of your existence. Everything else flows from there.

Now, loving Jesus will not be a problem when you know him as he truly is. So that is the place to begin, or for some of us, to return to after long wandering. We have quite an adventure before us, and the greatest treasure in the world to recover as our own. It will help to keep close the simplest of prayers:

Jesus, I ask you for you. For the real you.

Let us begin with a story.

CHAPTER ONE

THE PLAYFULNESS OF GOD AND THE POISON OF RELIGION

THE PLAYFULNESS OF GOD

This episode takes place a week or so *after* Jesus saunters out of the tomb he borrowed. The apostle John, one of Jesus' closest friends, recounts it:

Afterward Jesus appeared again to his disciples, by the Sea of Tiberias. It happened this way: Simon Peter, Thomas (called Didymus), Nathanael from Cana in Galilee, the sons of Zebedee, and two other disciples were together. "I'm going out to fish," Simon Peter told them, and they said, "We'll go with you." So they went out and got into the boat, but that night they caught nothing.

Early in the morning, Jesus stood on the shore, but the disciples did not realize that it was Jesus. He called out to them, "Friends, haven't you any fish?" "No," they answered. He said, "Throw your net on the right side of the boat and you will find some." When they did, they were unable to haul the net in because of the large number of fish.

Then the disciple whom Jesus loved said to Peter, "It is the Lord!" As soon as Simon Peter heard him say, "It is the Lord," he wrapped his outer garment around him (for he had taken it off) and jumped into the water. The other disciples followed in the boat, towing the net full of fish, for they were not far from shore, about a hundred yards. When they landed, they saw a fire of burning coals there with fish on it, and some bread.

Jesus said to them, "Bring some of the fish you have just caught." Simon Peter climbed aboard and dragged the net ashore. It was full of large fish, 153, but even with so many the net was not torn. Jesus said to them, "Come and have breakfast." (JOHN 21:1–12)

So many things are delicious about this story it's hard to know where to dive in.

First, the boys have gone fishing. Can you blame them? The events of the past two weeks have been, to say the least, overwhelming. The emotional high of the triumphal entry—palm branches waving, crowds shouting "Hosanna!"—it all crashed lower than anyone thought possible. Their beloved Jesus was tortured, executed, entombed. But then—fantastic beyond imagining—he appeared to them alive again. Twice. Though at this moment, they're not sure where he has gone off to. Not really sure what to do next, unable to endure one more agonizing moment waiting around the house, they do what any self-respecting angler who needs to get out and clear his head does: They go fishing. Apparently, fishing naked or darn close to it—notice that Peter needed to put his clothes back *on*.

Notice how *casually* Jesus enters the scene. His best friends don't even know its him. This is the resurrected Lord, mind you. Ruler of the heavens and the earth. Think Mount of Transfiguration. Jesus could have announced his risen presence on the beach with radiant glory. He knows there is nothing in the world that would help his mates more than to see him again. He certainly could have shouted in his commanding way, "It is I, the Lord! Come thou unto me!" He doesn't. He does the opposite—he "hides" himself a bit longer to let this play out. He simply stands on the shore, hands in his pockets like a tourist, and asks the question curious passersby always do of fishermen: "Catch anything?"

The nonchalance of the risen Christ here is absolutely intriguing. Whatever Jesus is up to, the moment is loaded for his next move.

Now, two more things are needed to set the stage properly.

First, what would you guess Jesus' mood is this particular morning? Surely he must be *happy*. The man has conquered death, ransomed mankind, been restored to his Father, his friends, and the world he made. Forever. He is in the afterglow of the greatest triumph of the greatest battle in the history of the cosmos. I'm going to venture that he is one mighty happy man. But not the fellas—up all night, nothing to show for it, bleary, half dead at the oars while the boat rocks back and forth, back and forth. They could use some cheering up.

Last, how did these—his closest brothers—first encounter Jesus? It was here, along the shore of this lake. Possibly this very spot, knowing how fishermen tend to keep their boat near a favorite hole.

That first compelling encounter also involved the fellas skunked after a night of fishing. It, too, began with a seemingly random instruction:

> "Put out into deep water, and let down the nets for a catch." ...
> When they had done so, they caught such a large number of fish that their nets began to break. So they signaled their part-ners in the other boat to come and help them, and they came and filled both boats so full that they began to sink. ... So they pulled their boats up on shore, left everything and followed him. (LUKE 5:4, 6–7, 11)

So, this has happened before.

That first miraculous catch—nets bursting, boats swamping—it must have felt like ages ago, after all that has unfolded. Or unraveled, depending on your point of view. But it was *their* story, the way they got pulled into this whole revolution. Most Christians can tell you in detail how they met Jesus, especially if it was a dramatic encounter. That payload was a story this inner circle no doubt talked about many times after, as guys will do, as *fishermen* will especially do. Sitting around their nightly fire, somebody brings it up with a smirk: "Peter, the look on your face was priceless," then, imitating Peter's reaction, "'Go away from me, Lord; I am a sinful man,'" and they all fall to cracking up about it again. (Luke 5:8)

My buddies and I used to make an annual fishing trip to the east-ern Sierra Nevada. Though our catches might not have been miracu-lous, we did haul in a scandalous load of fish, and in classic man fashion—campfires, canned beans, no showers. Except one year, we brought a guy named Bill who would take an hour every morning in camp to primp and preen and even put on cologne. We'd be in the car, laying on the horn, while Bill combed gel into his hair. Years after we'd rib him for it. All anyone needed to do was start the story with "Remember how Bill...," and sombody'd laugh, snort coffee through their nose, and the whole gang would be gasping for air again.

So here the famous disciples are, three years later. They've pulled another all-nighter. Off that same beach. The boys are skunked again. And Jesus does it again.

"Try the other side." Again the nets are bursting. It's how he lets them know it's him. This has all the wink of an inside joke, that rich treasure of friendship, the running gag between mates where over time all you need to do is start the first line and everyone cracks up all over again. "Try the other side." Another jackpot. Just like the good old days. Nothing more needs to be said—Peter is already in the water thrashing for shore.

Do you see the *playfulness* of Jesus?

His timing, the tension, his hiddenness, a touristlike question, the same lame suggestion from somebody they think knows nothing about fishing, then *bang!*—the catch. And the boys are hooked again. This is a beautiful story, made so much richer *because of* the playfulness of Jesus.

And by the way, that little detail John tosses in—that the catch was 153 fish, precisely—that, too, is a beautiful touch.

The net contained not "a boatload" of fish, nor "about a hundred and a half," nor "over a gross," but precisely "an hundred and fifty and three." This is, it seems to me, one of the most remarkable statistics ever computed. Consider the circumstances: this is *after* the crucifixion and the resurrection; Jesus is standing on the beach newly risen from the dead, and it is only the third time the disciples have seen him since the nightmare of Calvary. And yet we learn that in the net there were..."an hundred and fifty and three." How was this digit discovered? Mustn't it have happened thus: upon hauling the net to shore, the disciples squatted down by that immense, writhing fish pile and started tossing them into a second pile, painstakingly counting "one, two, three, four, five, six, seven..." all the way up to an hundred and fifty and three, while the newly risen Lord of Creation, the Sustainer of their beings, He who died for them and for Whom they would gladly die, stood waiting, ignored, till the heap of fish was quantified.[1]

Or, it might have gone like this: These retired fishermen, overcome with the joy of seeing Jesus, leave the writhing pile where it is, fully intending to get to it right after breakfast. Having had the cookout—which the risen Jesus grilled, by the way—one of them says, "Well, we oughta get that catch counted up," and a second says, "Yep," and Jesus, reaching for a last bite of roasted tilapia, says, "There's a hundred and fifty-three."

The boys smile at one another, realizing, *Oh yeah, right—we've got Jesus back.*

Any way you look at it, it is a beautiful story. Playful, funny, so human, so hopeful, so unreligious. And it is that particular quality that gives the passage its true character and gives us an essential for knowing Jesus as he really is. The man is not religious. If he were, the story would have taken place in a religious setting—the temple, perhaps, or at least a synagogue—and Jesus would have gathered them for a Bible study or prayer meeting. Jesus doesn't even show up at the temple after his resurrection. He's at the beach, catching his boys fishing, filling their empty nets and then having them to breakfast.

Now—why does this interpretation of the passage both relieve and trouble?

The relief comes in like a sea breeze on a muggy summer day suffocating with the smell of mud and dead fish. Because it is an answer to a question we didn't dare ask—that God himself knows how and when to be playful. With us. It's like a breath of fresh air.

But many readers are at the same time troubled because it also sounds a little irreverent. Which brings me to my second point.

THE POISON OF RELIGION

Jesus healed a man on a Sabbath. That pushed his enemies over the top. They decided to kill him. The account takes place early in the Gospel of Mark:

> Another time he went into the synagogue, and a man with a shriveled hand was there. Some of them were looking for a reason to accuse Jesus, so they watched him closely to see if he would heal him on the Sabbath. Jesus said to the man with the shriveled hand, "Stand up in front of everyone." Then Jesus asked them, "Which is lawful on the Sabbath: to do good or to do evil, to save life or to kill?" But they remained silent. He looked around at them in anger and, deeply distressed at their stubborn hearts, said to the man, "Stretch out your hand." He stretched it out, and his hand was completely restored. Then the Pharisees went out and began to plot with the Herodians how they might kill Jesus. (3:1–6)

Really. Because he healed a man on the Sabbath? What do we have here?

After all the nonsense that is repeated about Jesus being a gentle peacemaker, reading the Gospels is really quite a shock. We discover a Jesus who is in fact *frequently* embroiled in conflict—most of which he provokes himself (like healing on the Sabbath). And every single one of these clashes is with very religious people. Not one hostile encounter involves a "pagan." Not until the end, at least, when the Roman troopers get hold of him—but he was handed over by the religious establishment.

If you were reading the Gospels without bias or assumption, you would have no trouble whatsoever coming to believe that religion is the enemy—or in the hands of the enemy. Jesus' opponents are all people we would consider to be highly invested in doing religion right. They certainly considered themselves to be so.

You will want to keep this in mind if you would know Jesus, really.

For to come to know Jesus intimately, as he is, *as he wants to be known*, is to release a redemptive landslide in your life. There will be no stopping the goodness. The first purpose of your existence will be resolved, and from there you are set to fulfill all of God's other purposes for you. Now—do you really think that the enemy of our souls, the archenemy of Jesus Christ, is simply going to let that happen? Satan is far too subtle to rely on persecution alone. His most masterful works are works of *deception* (ask Adam and Eve about this when you see them). So the Deceiver deceives by means of *distortion*, and his favorite tool is to present a distorted Christ. Not so blatant as a bad fish, but through the respectable channels of religion.

Consider this one piece of evidence: millions of people who have spent years attending church, and yet they don't know God. Their heads are filled with stuffing *about* Jesus, but they do not experience him, not as the boys did on the beach. There are millions more who love Jesus Christ but experience him only occasionally, more often stumbling along short of the life he promised, like Lazarus still wrapped in his graveclothes.

Can anything be more diabolical?

If you sent someone you loved to school for a decade, yet they remained illiterate, how would you feel about the education? If you referred someone you loved to a doctor, yet despite years of treatment they not only failed to recover from their cancer but contracted HIV, hepatitis, and gangrene, what would you have to conclude about the treatment?

I am not making accusations; I am stating facts. There are noble churches and movements bringing Jesus to us. But alas, alas—they are the exception, not the rule.

Jesus healed a man on the Sabbath. His enemies decided to kill him. Do you really think that's over?! Why would that have ended with the time of Christ? Really now—it would be just a little arrogant for us to assume we could not fall under the same religious haze.

Thus George MacDonald, that old Scottish prophet, asks, "How have we learned Christ? It ought to be a startling thought, that we may have learned him wrong." It *is* a startling thought. "That must be far worse than not to have learned him at all: his place is occupied by a false Christ, hard to exorcise!"[2] Hard to exorcise, indeed, because religion gives the *impression* of having Christ, while it inoculates you from experiencing the real thing. Most wicked. If you want to destroy an economy, flood the market with counterfeit bills.

So the apostle John gives a last word of warning:

Dear friends, do not believe every spirit, but test the spirits to see whether they are from God, because many false prophets have gone out into the world. This is how you can recognize the Spirit of God: Every spirit that acknowledges that Jesus Christ has come in the flesh is from God, but every spirit that does not acknowledge Jesus is not from God. This is the spirit of the antichrist, which you have heard is coming and even now is already in the world. . . . This is how we recognize the Spirit of truth and the spirit of falsehood. (1 JOHN 4:1–3, 6)

A mighty important caution. But I'm afraid we read it with the same attention we give to the average preflight safety demonstration: "In the event of a water landing…" So, let's take it piece by piece. John says there is a Spirit of truth (that would be the Holy Spirit) and a spirit of falsehood (which he calls the spirit of the antichrist). He laments that many deceivers have infiltrated our world, animated by this spirit of falsehood. A sobering picture. He urges us to pay close attention, because that spirit works by presenting distorted images of Jesus.

Now—if John didn't think you could fall prey to it, he wouldn't have warned you about it. Before the ink was dry on the Gospels, the young church was swimming in this stuff.

Let me make this perfectly clear: The spirit of falsehood is often a very religious spirit. How else could it sell its deceptions? Over the past two thousand years, it has flooded the church with counterfeit currency. I'm not talking about only the blatant stuff—the Inquisition, witch trials, televangelists. Such repugnance does cause the world to turn away in disgust. A very effective technique. But while those forgeries have become obvious to us, consider—they were very convincing at the time.

For the religious spirit is like the flu—it is constantly adapting to the environment. It would be hard to hold a witch trial in our day. So what might it be in our time? Last week a friend heard his pastor say, "You can't know Jesus like you know your friends. He is altogether different from us." Blasphemy. You can know Jesus just as intimately as his first disciples did. Maybe more so. Jesus *came* to be known, for heaven's sake, came to make God known to us:

In the past God spoke to our forefathers through the prophets at many times and in various ways, but in these last days he has spoken to us by his Son....The Son is the radiance of God's glory and the exact representation of his being. (HEBREWS 1:1–3)

Jesus came to reveal God to us. He is the defining word on God— on what the heart of God is truly like, on what God is up to in the world, and on what God is up to in your life. An intimate encounter with Jesus is the most transforming experience of human existence. To know him as he is, is to come home. To have his life, joy, love, and presence cannot be compared. A true knowledge of Jesus is our greatest need and our greatest happiness. To be mistaken about him is the saddest mistake of all.

Now—he didn't go the lengths of the incarnation to then hide from us for the next two thousand years.

There is a popular "Let's get real and authentic" teaching that hopes to help us with our struggles by making it all right that God is distant, that we must struggle on with only a few whispers from him. And while that is comforting—sort of—does it really bring people to a regular experience of Jesus? That's what Christianity is supposed to do.

From the very first day, we were there, taking it all in—we heard it with our own ears, saw it with our own eyes, verified it with our own hands. The Word of Life appeared right before our eyes; we saw it happen! And now we're telling you in most sober prose that what we witnessed was, incredibly, this: The infinite Life of God himself took shape before us. We saw it, we heard it, and now we're telling you so you can experience it along with us, this experience of communion with the Father and his Son, Jesus Christ. (1 JOHN 1:1–3 The Message)

The records of Christ are written *so you can experience him as they did*, this intimate connection with the Father and the Son. John says that you can enjoy the same friendship with Jesus that he knew. For this Jesus came.

So, if you do not know Jesus as a person, know his remarkable *personality*—playful, cunning, fierce, impatient with all that is religious, kind, creative, irreverent, funny—you have been cheated.

If you do not experience Jesus intimately, daily, *in these very ways*, if you do not know the comfort of his actual presence, do not hear his voice speaking to you personally—you have been robbed.

If you do not know the power of his indwelling life in you, shaping your personality, healing your brokenness, enabling you to live as he did—*you have been plundered.*

This is why we pray,

Jesus, show me who you really are. I pray for the true you. I want the real you. I ask you for you. Spirit of God, free me in every way to know Jesus as he really is. Open my eyes to see him. Deliver me from everything false about Jesus and bring me what is true.

CHAPTER TWO

THE MISSING ESSENTIAL—HIS *PERSONALITY*

E-mail and texting have gotten me into a lot of trouble.

The reason is simple—those who receive my electronic missives cannot hear my tone of voice or see the expression on my face as they interpret my words. A very dangerous vacuum. Disembodied words have a way of being haunted. Too many times I've sent along something intended as playful, but without that twinkle in my eye or the slight grin on my face so essential to understanding my intentions, my readers have taken the playful comment seriously and been hurt by it. Sometimes I *have* intended a word of correction—but it was dashed off in a hurry, and again, without the smile and reassuring tone of voice so essential to convey my heart, the message came across as harsh.

This is the vacuum many of us bring to the Gospels.

Without Jesus' tone of voice, what was in his eyes, the lift of an eyebrow, a suppressed smile, a tilt of the head, an unflinching gaze, we misinterpret a great deal of what we find there. Reading the Gospels without the personality of Jesus is like watching television with the sound turned off. You get a very dry, two-dimensional person doing strange, undecipherable things. Take this story as one example:

A Canaanite woman from that vicinity came to him, crying out, "Lord, Son of David, have mercy on me! My daughter is suffering terribly from demon-possession." Jesus did not answer a word. So his disciples came to him and urged him, "Send her away, for she keeps crying out after us." He answered, "I was sent only to the lost sheep of Israel." The woman came and knelt before him. "Lord, help me!" she said. He replied, "It is not right to take the children's bread and toss it to their dogs." "Yes, Lord," she said, "but even the dogs eat the crumbs that fall from their masters' table." Then Jesus answered, "Woman, you have great faith! Your request is granted." And her daughter was healed from that very hour. (MATTHEW 15:22–28)

Oh, my. What do we make of this? "I'm not here for you dogs?!" Many good people read this passage, cringe, and walk away with a subtle conviction that Jesus is a harder man than they thought, *And well, I guess that hardness is good somehow.* Some go on to build theologies based on his hardness. But of course, if Jesus was being *playful*— well, that would change everything.

Seriously now—what comes to mind when you think of Jesus? It might be good to stop and do an inventory. Is Jesus near—or far? Is he close at hand, right here at your elbow, or distant and engaged in loftier things? Does he have a sense of humor? What words would you use to describe him? If you gathered the many books on Jesus and combed them for the words used most often to describe him, you can guess beforehand what you would get: *loving* and *compassionate*.

Beautiful qualities, and certainly true of Jesus. But two-dimensional. Especially when we color these virtues with religious tones. Love turns sickly sweet and compassion soft and limp. How is it possible to genuinely and consistently love anything so two-dimensional? Loving and compassionate—it's like trying to love a get-well card.

Young writers are encouraged to "find their voice," because it is *personality* that distinguishes a good novel from a phone book. Both are filled with words. Only one is worth reading. Personality is what distinguishes real music from elevator music. Both are made up of notes; only one is worth listening to. Think of the people you have most loved and trusted—*why* did you love and trust them so? Was it because of one quality, or was it the funky, endearing combination of all those qualities that together made them who they were?

Personality is what makes someone some*one* and not everyone, or anyone.

You simply cannot love Lincoln or Charlemagne like you love your closest and dearest friend. Though historic figures may be admirable, you cannot love them because you do not *know* them. They are far too removed from your personal experience to win or sustain your true love. Actual experiences of their personalities is something no one ever really gets. But when it comes to friends, family, lovers, we love them because of who they are—*because* of their personality. My goodness, we love our pets because of their personalities—the fact that your cat sits on your head and licks your ear to wake you, or that your dog has a taste for gingersnaps and underwear.

Last May I had the opportunity, while in London, to visit the National Gallery. Loving art, and being with two of my sons—one of whom is an art major—I was excited to spend hours there. I loved the

Van Gogh, the Monet, the Rembrandt paintings and more. But there was one massive disappointment. No, it was more than disappointment. Massive frustration. I did not see one portrait of Christ, in all the famous works of him, that came anywhere close to depicting Jesus as he really is. Not one. They are all of a wispy, pale Jesus, looking haunted, a ghostlike figure floating along through life making strange gestures and undecipherable statements.

The Nativity scenes were particularly ridiculous. The classic art depicting the infant—themes now repeated on Christmas cards and in the crèche scenes displayed in churches and on suburban coffee tables—portrays a rather mature baby, very white, radiantly clean as no baby is ever clean, arms outstretched to reassure the nervous adults around him, intelligent, without need, halo glowing, conscious with an adult consciousness. Superbaby. This infant clearly never pooped his diapers. He looks ready to take up the prime ministership.

Why did it make me angry?

Because when we lose his *personality*, we lose Jesus.

It's a little ironic that in a sophisticated visual age like ours we still cling to a two-dimensional Jesus. Such is the power of the religious fog. I've been doing a good bit of reading in preparation for writing this book, and the chorus of voices when it comes to the personality of Jesus is unanimous. Everyone talks about his "great acts of humility, faith, and compassion." What about his great acts of playfulness, or cunning? What about his brilliance, his wit, his irreverence, the scandalous freedom with which Jesus lives, his exasperation and impatience? Not to mention his humanity; we have nearly forgotten he was a man.

Good grief—your hamster seems to have a more fully developed personality than most portraits of Jesus.

Furthermore, the loss of personality confounds our imitation of

Christ. What happens is, our particular brand of church seizes upon one or two of his virtues as the essence of Christ for us to follow. Justice. Mercy. Righteousness. Whatever. You cannot live a life on one quality any more than you can speak intelligently using one word. Meanwhile, we continue to sound on about the love and compassion of Jesus, like the village idiot banging one note on a piano. After a while the world turns away. Can you blame them? Alas—if only Jesus' followers shared his personality. That one shift alone would correct so many of the ridiculous and horrifying things that pass for popular Christianity.

What is missing in our Gospel reading—and in our attempts to "read" what Jesus is saying and doing in our own lives right now, this week—is his *personality*, undraped by religion. Let's see if we can find it.

CHAPTER THREE

IS JESUS REALLY *PLAYFUL*?

Our golden retriever has invented a game he plays by himself. Oban will find in the yard the largest rock he can carry, gingerly bring it to the top of the hill, where he drops it. Then, positioned uphill of the rock, he gives it a little nudge with his nose, sending it bouncing down like a rabbit trying to get away and him bounding after. Then he pounces. Which of course ends the chase, so he'll release his prize, send it off with another push, dash down after, crashing through the bushes, nudging it along to give it speed, then seizing it with another pounce. He'll lie there triumphantly for a moment or two, panting, a lion with its prey between its paws, till he gets that wild look in his eye and starts the whole game over.

It makes us laugh every time. And no one taught him to do this. He came that way. God created him so.

It might seem an odd place to begin a search for Jesus, but this is very close to where John begins his Gospel: "Through him all things were made; without him nothing was made that has been made" (John 1:3).

We have a good bit of rubble to remove when it comes to knowing Jesus *as he is*, so let us begin where John does—with creation. You can learn a lot about an artist by the work he or she leaves behind—the hubris of Hemingway, for example, is difficult to hide even if he wanted to; so is the tortured darkness of Edgar Allan Poe. The whimsy of Chagall shimmers through his paintings, as does the radiant genius of Van Gogh. The personality of the artist leaks through their work. God included. He reveals himself through nature, as the Scriptures testify.

This will open up wonders for you about the personality of Jesus—look at his works of art.

I was sitting out back yesterday morning sipping coffee, watching the young chipmunks chase one another at breakneck speeds across the deck. One clever daredevil, hoping to get the advantage, jumped up on the fence rail and continued the chase from above, leaping at the last moment upon his littermate like a Hollywood stuntman. This morning one of them adopted a new strategy. The little rascal found an ambush spot, clinging from the side of the house, where he waited for his playmate to wander by unawares; he then pounced, and the two somersaulted off the deck and into the grass, squealing. Only to dash off and do it again. And again.

Now—what does this tell us about the personality of Jesus, who created these little dynamos with striped masks and boundless enthusiasm? What do they say about his heart? Polar-bear cubs will hurl themselves down snowy hillsides headfirst and upside down, just for fun. Spinner dolphins love to romp in the bow-wake of a boat, cavorting, leaping into the air and, well, spinning. Otters play tag. Our horses play tug-of-war with a stick—which is really quite funny when you think of how nobly a horse normally likes to carry himself.

Who gave your puppy his *impishness*, as he snatches your slipper and races round the house with you in tow? God is more playful than we are. Or we are greater at something than he is—a claim no one would dare.

My boys are in their late teens now, and as such it is as easy to get them to do some chores as it is to coax ketchup from a bottle. Several days ago we badgered them into cleaning the windows. Come dinnertime, our family seated round the table, the brothers began—as all brothers do—to give each other grief about the day's work. Sam and Luke had each taken halves of a divided window in the dining room; Sam was now bragging about how much cleaner his side was, appealing to the evidence like a trial attorney. We turned our attention toward the window in question—at that exact moment a robin smacked into Luke's pane, fell to the ground stunned, shook itself, and flew away. We looked at one another, mouths open, eyebrows raised, and burst into laughter.

Nature had voted. *God* had voted.

His timing could not have been richer. "Whose window is clean? Who slacked on the job?" *Thwack*. Brilliant. You couldn't have asked for a more choice reply. The whole episode was hysterical. Now, if you have any belief in the sovereignty of God, you discover that these moments are *orchestrated*. Not a sparrow hits a window without your Father knowing it, or something like that.

Haven't you seen something in nature that made you laugh? Perhaps you did not make the connection—that you were *meant* to laugh. That it was God who made you laugh. That he laughed with you. Now you know something very important about Jesus.

Elton Trueblood conducted a good bit of research in order to write a biblical defense of Jesus' playfulness in his book *The Humor of Christ*. It is a very thorough, scholarly, and dry book. Which is actually pretty funny—a humorless book about God's sense of humor. What does it say of us, or of our church culture, that such a book even *needs* to be written? That we have to go to great lengths to wonder if God laughs? How far have we strayed from his heart, his personality?

Does Jesus have a sense of humor? Well, he created laughter.

And think of the crowd he dined with. These rabble-rousers quickly earned Jesus a reputation as a drunkard and a glutton, and it wasn't because they served water and crackers. This was a wild group, and surely such a crowd got rolling in laughter from time to time, if only from the joy they were experiencing being with Jesus. Now, surely the creator of these colorful characters didn't sit there frowning, looking pious, Mr. Killjoy, Mr. I'm-Above-All-This. Imagine his own happiness at having these very lost sheep back at his side.

But the religious tight-shorts didn't like it one bit. They constantly griped about it.

Last Christmas a friend sent me a gift; it was a coffee mug with a classic picture of Jesus on it, and below the famous line "Jesus Saves." When you pour hot drinks into the mug, the imagery changes—Christ no longer has a beard, and the expression says, "Jesus shaves." My son Luke asked me hesitantly, "What do you think Jesus thinks about that?" Let me ask you, my reader—what do *you* think? Remove Jesus from the equation for a moment—how do you feel about people who must always be serious, who demand that everyone around them always be serious? And what about sour types who can never, ever tolerate a playful tease?

Can Jesus enjoy a joke at his own expense? If not, what kind of person is he? I told Luke, "I think he thinks it's hysterical." But we have to hide the mug when certain members of our church stop by.

Laughter is from God. This one quality alone might save us from the religious veil that forever tries to come in and cloud our perception of Jesus.

Keep in mind now—*Isaac* means "laughter." And who was it that gave him this unforgettable name? It was the Lord.

The place to start is with a woman laughing. She is an old woman, and, after a lifetime in the desert, her face is cracked and rutted like a six-month drought. She hunches her shoulders around her ears and starts to shake. She squinnies her eyes shut, and her laughter is all China teeth and wheeze and tears running down as she rocks hard back and forth in her kitchen chair. She is laughing because she is pushing ninety-one hard and has just been told she is going to have a baby. Even though it was an angel who told her, she can't control herself, and her husband can't control himself either. He keeps a straight face a few seconds longer than she does, but he ends by cracking up, too...

The old woman's name is Sarah, of course, and the old man's name is Abraham, and they are laughing at the idea of a baby's being born in the geriatric ward and Medicare's picking up the tab. They are laughing because the angel not only seems to believe it but seems to expect them to believe it too. They are laughing because with part of themselves they do believe it.... They are laughing because if by some crazy chance it should just happen to come true, then they really would have something to laugh about.[1]

Old enough to be great-grandparents, Abraham and Sarah are swapping the walker for a stroller. It's just too much. The arthritic patriarch and his wrinkled wife try to hide their laughter from the living God. He seals the humor of the whole thing himself by naming Isaac for them. Laughter.

After all—it was *God* who gave us a sense of humor. Do you really think Jesus came to take it away?

Maybe if we allow Jesus the playfulness we see in his creation, we can then see him at play in the Gospels. Perhaps it will help us unlock some of these otherwise perplexing stories.

> After Jesus and his disciples arrived in Capernaum, the collectors of the two-drachma tax came to Peter and asked, "Doesn't your teacher pay the temple tax?" "Yes, he does," he replied. When Peter came into the house, Jesus was the first to speak. "What do you think, Simon?" he asked. "From whom do the kings of the earth collect duty and taxes—from their own sons or from others?" "From others," Peter answered. "Then the sons are exempt," Jesus said to him. "But so that we may not offend them, go to the lake and throw out your line. Take the first fish you catch; open its mouth and you will find a four-drachma coin. Take it and give it to them for my tax and yours." (MATTHEW 17:24–27)

What? This is a mighty strange little story. Why in the world does Jesus send Peter off on a quest right out of an Irish fairy tale? "The Apostle and the Salmon of Gold." We're talking about a few dollars here. What is with the fishing trip? If you remove the actual personality of Jesus from the scene—and insert that religious, ethereal, ghostlike personality gazing off into realms unknown, the image of Christ conjured up by so many paintings and Sunday school art—you wind up with some pretty bizarre interpretations. That the open mouth of the fish, as one commentator has it, represents the open hearts of people who will receive the gospel as Peter becomes, after the resurrection, a fisher of men. An exercise of hermeneutical contortion worthy of Cirque du Soleil.

Contorted interpretations based upon religiously bizarre images only serve to push Christ further off into the ethosphere. "And by their fruit you shall know them," warned Jesus (see Matt. 7:16).

But with his personality front and center, these stories take on a richness we have missed.

Peter has taken an enormous risk hitching his wagon to Jesus. The little band of minstrels have passed the raised-eyebrows stage and are about to enter the period of opposition to Christ—the pitchforks-and-torches stage. Peter is confronted by the elders of his own village with a troubling question. He comes into the house visibly shaken, and sees his master standing at the counter chopping vegetables. There is a moment of silence, while the pang of doubt shoots through his mind: *Perhaps the Master is not as righteous as we thought; he does not seem to keep the Law.* Jesus does not look up; he simply says, "What do you think, Simon...?"

"Peter, I'll tell you what I need you to do..." He sends the fisherman fishing. He gives him time to sort things out. He shows him there are higher laws to live by. Jesus has a sense of humor. Without a deep confidence in that, the story is simply bizarre. But with that understanding, it is a beautiful and very human and also immensely funny story. The fruit of which is only to make us love him more.

And you shall know them by their fruit.

Here's another wonderful moment when Jesus' tone of voice means everything:

The next day Jesus decided to leave for Galilee. Finding Philip, he said to him, "Follow me." Philip, like Andrew and Peter, was from the town of Bethsaida. Philip found Nathanael and told him, "We have found the one Moses wrote about in the Law, and about whom the prophets also wrote—Jesus of Nazareth, the son of Joseph." "Nazareth! Can anything good come from there?" Nathanael asked. "Come and see," said Philip. When Jesus saw Nathanael approaching, he said of him, "Here is a true Israelite, in whom there is nothing false." "How do you know me?" Nathanael asked. Jesus answered, "I saw you while you were still under the fig tree before Philip called you." Then Nathanael declared, "Rabbi, you are the Son of God; you are the King of Israel." Jesus said, "You believe because I told you I saw you under the fig tree. You shall see greater things than that." (JOHN 1:43–50)

These guys are meeting Jesus for the first time. Keep in mind now that Jesus knows what is about to unfold, all that these lads will be swept up into—feeding the five thousand, commanding the storm to cease, raising Lazarus from the dead. Nathanael says, "How in the world do you even know me? We've never seen each other before." Jesus says, casually, "Oh, I saw you—under the fig tree before Philip came to get you." Nathanael hits his knees: "You are the son of God, the King of Israel!" Jesus' response is priceless: "You believe because I told you I saw you under the fig tree?" There has to be a couple of raised eyebrows and a suppressed smile on his face. *Wow—you're easily impressed.* And then, knowing what Nathanael is going to behold, he has to chuckle just a bit when he says, "Oh...you'll see greater things than that."

I'm remembering a story from last summer. My sons and I were on the first leg of a five-day backpacking trip into a wilderness area we'd never visited before. We'd been on the trail only forty-five minutes or so, but already I am bringing up the rear (I am the old goat now). I'm looking around, taking in the sights, when I notice moose sign on the trail—droppings, tracks. Not fresh, but still, it didn't even cross my mind that we might be in moose country. I love moose. Seeing one is a celebration for me. With a hesitant hopefulness, I prayed, "Wow, Jesus... it would be awesome if we could see a moose sometime during this trip!" I'm thinking several days from now, once we're into the back country, and maybe then only from a mile away. Jesus' immediate reply was deadpan: *You will.* Count one thousand one... one thousand two... one thousand *bam*. There in front of us, sixty yards away, is a moose grazing in the meadow.

His comic timing could not have been more exquisite.

Recalling Jesus' playfulness with the guys when he did a "take two" of the miraculous catch, have another look at the classic "Emmaus Road" story:

> Now that same day [Resurrection Sunday] two of them were going to a village called Emmaus, about seven miles from Jerusalem. They were talking with each other about everything that had happened. As they talked and discussed these things with each other, Jesus himself came up and walked along with them; but they were kept from recognizing him. He asked them, "What are you discussing together as you walk along?" They stood still, their faces downcast. One of them, named Cleopas, asked him, "Are you only a visitor to Jerusalem and do not know the things that have happened there in these days?" "What things?" he asked. (LUKE 24:13–19)

Pause. You have got to be kidding. Here are two of Jesus' disciples as grief-stricken as human hearts can be. They think he's dead. They think it's all over. If any moment cried out for good news from Jesus, it was this one. Yet again, how *casually* he enters the scene, this time as a traveler with a flight to catch. He just sort of huffs up alongside, again "hiding" himself as he later does on the beach, to let this play out. He asks what they're so upset about—can you believe it?! Cleopas can't. How is it possible that this stranger could have missed the things rocking Jerusalem the past few days? "What things?" Jesus inquires.

Ummm . . . if anyone knows "what things," it is Jesus. These are *his* "things" for heaven's sake, his most important things ever. He *feigns ignorance*?! The story continues:

"About Jesus of Nazareth," they replied. "He was a prophet, powerful in word and deed before God and all the people. The chief priests and our rulers handed him over to be sentenced to death, and they crucified him; but we had hoped that he was the one who was going to redeem Israel. And what is more, it is the third day since all this took place. In addition, some of our women amazed us. They went to the tomb early this morning but didn't find his body. They came and told us that they had seen a vision of angels, who said he was alive. Then some of our companions went to the tomb and found it just as the women had said, but him they did not see." (vv. 19–24)

Remember now—what is Jesus' overall mood this particular Sunday morning? Just a few hours ago he walked out of the grave with the keys to hell swinging on his belt and the redemption of mankind in his pocket. Would it be safe to say he is cheerful? Maybe even excited?

Jubilant? Christ is about as happy as anyone has ever been in the history of the world. But so far he has appeared only to Mary Magdalene. Isn't the moment crying out for him to reveal himself to these shell-shocked followers: "Look—it's me! I'm alive! Everything is going to be okay! Rejoice! Tell the world!"

He doesn't.

He carries on with the disguise, apparently for some time, holding forth on highlights from the Old Testament as the three tramp along. Then comes this unbelievable moment:

> As they approached the village to which they were going, Jesus acted as if he were going farther. But they urged him strongly, "Stay with us, for it is nearly evening; the day is almost over." So he went in to stay with them. (vv. 28–29)

He *acted as if* he were going farther?! "Well, nice talking to you chaps. So sorry for your loss. Hope things turn out. But I've got to get going." What in the world? Christ takes up the role of a thespian, pretending to have to move on, so that they must *beg* him to stay?! Oh, all right. If you insist. "When he was at the table with them, he took bread, gave thanks, broke it and began to give it to them. Then their eyes were opened and they recognized him, and he disappeared from their sight" (vv. 31–32). Poof. See ya.

What do you make of this story? Jesus' behavior is either (a) bizarre; (b) meant to drive home some obscure spiritual lesson, which, taking in the timing (the *first* thing he does after resurrecting?) and his playacting, is even *more* bizarre; or (c) playful. Given that this is the God of a playful creation on his resurrection morn, he who has been so playful with his followers in their years together, whom we see playing the inside joke on his closest friends a week from now, I'm putting my money on playful.

How have we missed this? Ask yourself, *Is this the Jesus of my friends? My church? Is this the Jesus we pray to? Is this what I look to experience from Jesus?*

CHAPTER FOUR

FIERCE INTENTION

From that time on Jesus began to explain to his disciples that he must go to Jerusalem and suffer many things at the hands of the elders, chief priests and teachers of the law, and that he must be killed and on the third day be raised to life. Peter took him aside and began to rebuke him. "Never, Lord!" he said. "This shall never happen to you!" Jesus turned and said to Peter, "Get behind me, Satan! You are a stumbling block to me; you do not have in mind the things of God, but the things of men." (MATTHEW 16:21–23)

Hold on now—this doesn't sound very playful.

What are we to make of the sudden mood changes that erupt from Jesus like thunder from a clear sky? If your children acted this way, you'd send them to their rooms. Whatever we have here, we certainly don't have a man of mild emotion or two-dimensional passivity.

For some reason we keep forgetting that Jesus is operating in enemy territory. We project into the Gospel stories a pastoral backdrop, the quaint charm of a Middle Eastern travel brochure—picturesque villages, bustling markets, smiling children—and Jesus wandering through it all like a son come home from college. We forget the context of his life and mission. His story begins with *genocide*—the massacre of the innocents, Herod's attempt to murder Jesus by ordering the systematic execution of all young boys around Bethlehem. I've never seen this included in any crèche scene, ever. Who could bear it? You must picture ethnic cleansing as the twentieth century saw in Bosnia, Rwanda, Burma. Atrocity, the ground soaked with the blood of children who five minutes earlier were laughing and playing.

God the Father, knowing this is about to strike, sends an angel to warn Joseph:

An angel of the Lord appeared to Joseph in a dream. "Get up," he said, "take the child and his mother and escape to Egypt. Stay there until I tell you, for Herod is going to search for the child to kill him." So he got up, took the child and his mother during the night and left for Egypt, where he stayed until the death of Herod. (MATTHEW 2:13–15)

The little family flees the country under cover of darkness, like fugitives. The Father's strategy is intriguing—surely God could have simply taken Herod out. Or sent angels to surround the holy family. Why must they run for their lives? It ought to make you think twice about how God goes about his plans in this world. But let us continue with the facts—an angel in the night, a flight in the dark, hiding south of the border like outlaws. Thus begins a dangerous game of cat and mouse:

> Jesus went around in Galilee, purposely staying away from Judea because the Jews there were waiting to take his life. (JOHN 7:1)

> The Pharisees went out and plotted how they might kill Jesus. Aware of this, Jesus withdrew from that place. (MATTHEW 12:14–15)

> Again they tried to seize him, but he escaped their grasp. Then Jesus went back across the Jordan to the place where John had been baptizing in the early days. (JOHN 10:39–40)

Surely you see that Jesus was a *hunted* man?

We cannot understand his actions, nor taste the richness of his personality until we set them within context—the man is operating deep behind enemy lines. This colors his extraordinary movements across the pages of the Gospels and helps to strip away that benevolent religious fog that continues to creep into our reading. It also gives depth and poignancy to moments of self-disclosure such as, "The Son of Man has no place to lay his head" (Matt. 8:20). Because he was hunted.

But is it not more true to say that he is the Hunter?

As Jesus steps out from behind those thirty years of almost total obscurity into the task set before him, both men and demons begin to feel his fierce intention:

> He went down to Capernaum, a town in Galilee, and on the Sabbath began to teach the people. They were amazed at his

teaching, because his message had authority. In the synagogue there was a man possessed by a demon, an evil spirit. He cried out at the top of his voice, "Ha! What do you want with us, Jesus of Nazareth? Have you come to destroy us? I know who you are—the Holy One of God!" "Be quiet!" Jesus said sternly. "Come out of him!" Then the demon threw the man down before them all and came out without injuring him. All the people were amazed and said to each other, "What is this teaching? With authority and power he gives orders to evil spirits and they come out!" (LUKE 4:31–36)

You cannot appreciate the difficulty of this till you've tried it yourself. Most of us wouldn't walk into a dark alley if we could avoid it. Early in his novel *Perelandra*, C. S. Lewis tells the story of a man called to help a friend on a very important task—one that is opposed by dark powers. As he leaves the train station and begins his trek to his friend's cottage in a fading twilight, he encounters that Opposition:

"Go back, go back," it whispered to me, "send him a wire, tell him you were ill, say you'll come some other time—anything." The strength of the feeling astonished me. I stood still for a few moments telling myself not to be a fool, and when I finally resumed my walk I was wondering whether this might be the beginning of a nervous breakdown.[1]

He passes an abandoned factory that looks "unbelievably ominous."[2] Fear slithers in. He is shot through with doubts about his friend. Then doubts about his view of the universe. Then more thoughts about having a nervous breakdown, which all seem confirmed by the swirling chaos in his mind and emotions. He wonders if he might be going mad.

I was past the dead factory now, down in the fog, where it was very cold. Then came a moment—the first one—of absolute terror and I had to bite my lips to keep myself from screaming. It was only a cat that had run across the road, but I found myself completely unnerved. "Soon you will really be screaming," said my inner tormentor. "Running round and round, screaming, and you won't be able to stop it." . . .

At all events I *can't* really describe how I reached the front door of the cottage. Somehow or other, despite the loathing and dismay that pulled me back and a sort of invisible wall of resistance that met me in the face, fighting for each step, and almost shrieking as a harmless spray of the hedge touched my face, I managed to get through the gate and up the little path. And there I was, drumming on the door and wringing the handle and shouting to him to let me in as if my life depended on it.[3]

An account so reliably written it had to have been drawn from personal experience. Many of you have endured something similar, if only in nightmares. And this poor fellow was merely trying to make it from the station to the cottage. Jesus walks right up to people foaming at the mouth in full-blown demonic possession and confronts the ancient spirits directly. Very intentional. Quite fierce.

Then comes the thunderstorm at the temple.

The Passover of the Jews was near, and Jesus went up to Jerusalem. In the temple he found people selling cattle, sheep, and doves, and the money changers seated at their tables. Making a whip of cords, he drove all of them out of the temple, both the sheep and the cattle. He also poured out the coins of the money changers and overturned their tables. He told those who were selling the doves, "Take these things out of here! Stop making my Father's house a marketplace!" His disciples remembered that it was written, "Zeal for your house will consume me." (JOHN 2:13–17 NRSV)

In two verses he empties the temple, a report that reads like the crack of a bullwhip. But take the action slowly. First, Jesus observes the shenanigans, and it makes him furious. Then he takes the time to make a weapon. Where did he get these cords? That required some looking around. Having found them, he had the patience and forethought to weave them together effectively to make a usable whip— he knows what it takes to move large, sedentary cattle and self-righteous profiteers. There's time enough here to cool off if this is merely an outburst of anger. But no, this is a planned and sustained aggression. (Particularly unsettling for pacifists.)

Following the flow of the text, it says he then used that whip to drive *all* of them out of the temple, both the sheep and the cattle. The livestock would have been kept in some sort of corral; they would have been standing for hours, languid, sleepy. An angry man flying upon them with a whip would ignite panic. Mass panic. Animals feed upon one another's fear in seconds. Picture cattle and sheep running for their lives, crashing down the corrals, their hooves sliding frantically on the tiles, making them even more desperate. We have a stampede here.

It then says he *poured out* the coins of the money changers and sent their tables tumbling. The money changers—think "men who make their living through extortion"—are reported to have been sitting at those tables. How easy is it to move carefully and quickly from a sitting position while removing your legs from the table that is being overturned in front of you? More panic. Meanwhile, the coins—Jesus doesn't permit them to gather their money and move off in an orderly fashion. He *dumps* the coins, scatters them. This is explosive. You've probably had a small handful of change fall off a counter—they burst in every direction like a jar of marbles. Imagine the chaos of hundreds and hundreds of coins erupting off the stone floors.

Now, layer all this together. The animals would have panicked in every direction, their keepers running after them, shouting, trying to get control, which only incinerates the panic. Add the greedy money changers scrambling around on the ground grasping at their careening coins. Imagine the *noise*—bellowing of frightened livestock mingled with the crashing of corrals, tables, coins, and the angry shouts of the incensed men. Over this, the shouts of Jesus. It is absolute pandemonium. Someone screaming "fire" in a casino would not be far from the reality.

This is a fierce, intentional man to be sure. But his passions are neither reckless nor momentary. In the midst of the fury there is the touching tenderness toward the doves—these were in cages. If Christ were to hurl them to the floor as he did the tables, the birds—innocent as, well, doves—they would be hurt. So he commands them to be removed.

Could a small, unintimidating figure accomplish such a sustained riot? To pull off driving "all of them out of the temple" would require more than a few seconds and repeated blows. This is a sustained assault. If a frail man with a meek voice tried this, he'd be logjammed by the sheer number and inertia of the traffic. Jesus is a locomotive, a juggernaut. For all practical purposes here, he *is* the bull in the china shop.

This is our Jesus.

But is this the Jesus of our worship songs? The religious fog sneaks in to obscure Jesus with lines comparing him to, "a rose trampled on the ground." Helpless, lovely Jesus. Vegetarian, pacifist, tranquil. Oh, wait—that was Gandhi. Not Jesus.

Can you picture Gandhi or Buddha storming into the polling place of a local election, shouting, overturning tables, sending the participants fleeing? Now throw a small carnival into the mix, which they also need to rout. Impossible. Whoever did this would have to be really committed to clear the building. Fierce and intentional.

This is a breathtaking quality—*especially* when compared to our present age where doubt masquerades as humility, passivity cloaks as rest, and emasculated indecision poses as laid-back enlightenment.

Oh, Jesus could be soft, and he certainly was humble, but his fierce intentionality is riveting to watch. Look at him before Lazarus's tomb:

On his arrival, Jesus found that Lazarus had already been in the tomb for four days.... When Mary reached the place where Jesus was and saw him, she fell at his feet and said, "Lord, if you had been here, my brother would not have died." When Jesus saw her weeping, and the Jews who had come along with her also weeping, he was deeply moved in spirit and troubled. (JOHN 11:17, 32–33)

This expression "deeply moved in spirit and troubled" seems unhelpfully vague. I'm "deeply moved" when someone remembers my birthday. An Oxford don who loses his notes is "troubled." We're not even close to the true nature of his mood yet. The root of the Greek word here means "to snort in anger," like a warhorse. Peterson therefore translates it, "a deep anger welled up within him" (John

11:33 The Message). Yes, that's better; of course it did. This is the Prince of Life, who came that we might have life—what do you suppose his personal attitude is toward death? And here, the death of a close friend? I hate death. I think I hate it more than anything else in all the world. Jesus has mighty strong feelings about it, too. "Deeply moved" doesn't mean someone had to catch his arm and help him toward the casket, Jesus overcome with sorrow.

Something fierce is rising up in him. A second round of this warhorse anger wells up:

> Jesus, once more deeply moved, came to the tomb. It was a cave with a stone laid across the entrance. "Take away the stone," he said. "But, Lord," said Martha, the sister of the dead man, "by this time there is a bad odor, for he has been there four days." Then Jesus said, "Did I not tell you that if you believed, you would see the glory of God?" So they took away the stone. Then Jesus looked up and said, "Father, I thank you that you have heard me. I knew that you always hear me, but I said this for the benefit of the people standing here, that they may believe that you sent me." When he had said this, Jesus called in a loud voice, "Lazarus, come out!" (vv. 38–43)

Oh, to have heard this command, heard the mightiness in his voice. John uses the word *loud* to describe it; he uses this very same word to describe the ferocity of a storm that nearly sank their boat. Apparently, Jesus' command here reminded John of the intensity of a storm. Jesus doesn't ask Lazarus to come out; he doesn't suggest he do. He commands him to life with the rumble of thunder and the crack of lightning. Obediently, Lazarus comes hopping out like a mummy:

The dead man came out, his hands and feet wrapped with strips of linen, and a cloth around his face. Jesus said to them, "Take off the grave clothes and let him go." (v. 44)

Jesus finishes his business here with the very businesslike order to "take off the grave clothes and let him go," like a hostage negotiator who has just freed a victim.

G. K. Chesterton conducted something of a personal experiment to see what the overall impression would be if a person simply read the Gospels without any previous information regarding Jesus. What he found surprised him:

It is full of sudden gestures evidently significant except that we hardly know what they signify; of enigmatic silences; of ironical replies. The outbreaks of wrath, like storms above our atmosphere, do not seem to break out exactly where we should expect them, but to follow some higher weather-chart of their own.[4]

Oh, but they do make sense, when you understand that this is a man on a mission. That the same man who could be so playful is also a man on fire. If you would know Jesus, you must know that this—his fierce intentionality—is essential to his personality.

Nature bears witness. Picture an African lion, stalking through tall grass, closing in on its prey—the ruthless focus, the vigilant keenness. Or the gaze of a silverback gorilla when he turns to confront an intruder crossing the hidden boundary of his band. How about a mother brown bear when her cubs are threatened? Six hundred pounds of unrelenting fury. Now imagine you are watching one of these scenes not on the nature channel but from thirty feet away. Oh, yes, we find a very fierce intentionality in nature—reflecting the personality of the Artist.

Knowing this—*delighting* in this—helps us delight in his highly provocative actions regarding the Sabbath. There is nothing like arrogant religious falsehood to arouse this part of Jesus:

> On a Sabbath Jesus was teaching in one of the synagogues, and a woman was there who had been crippled by a spirit for eighteen years. She was bent over and could not straighten up at all. When Jesus saw her, he called her forward and said to her, "Woman, you are set free from your infirmity." Then he put his hands on her, and immediately she straightened up and praised God. Indignant because Jesus had healed on the Sabbath, the synagogue ruler said to the people, "There are six days for work. So come and be healed on those days, not on the Sabbath."
>
> The Lord answered him, "You hypocrites! Doesn't each of you on the Sabbath untie his ox or donkey from the stall and lead it out to give it water? Then should not this woman, a daughter of Abraham, whom Satan has kept bound for eighteen long years, be set free on the Sabbath day from what bound her?" When he said this, all his opponents were humiliated, but the people were delighted with all the wonderful things he was doing. (LUKE 13:10–17)

There is nothing so suffocating as religious legalism. Here, in the one place this woman can hope for freedom, she is denied for eighteen years. Jesus is disgusted with it. He publicly humiliates the defenders of this sanctified bondage. His action isn't exactly going to ingratiate him with the authorities. I doubt very much "Willing to publicly humiliate Pharisees" is on any requirement list for pastoral candidates; I doubt it ought to be. This sort of thing takes a rare holiness to accomplish righteously. But the people are cheering, and well they should.

And then there is the story of subduing the storm I referred to earlier, and immediately after, the encounter with Legion. In all three synoptic Gospels, these two stories are linked—a frightening storm, and then a frightening demoniac. In all three accounts, Jesus—who was sleeping in the stern of the sinking boat—rises to confront the tempest like a drill sergeant: "Quiet! Be still!" Now, why does he need to *rebuke* the storm? The word—*epitimao*—is the same used when Jesus commands foul spirits to come out of people. Fascinating—the storm needed to be rebuked. The very next episode in all three synoptics finds Christ stepping on shore to confront Legion.

He frees the man, the locals rage against Jesus, and he gets right back in the boat and returns to the other side. Did he go to all that effort for one man? It ended up that way. And Jesus did say something about leaving the ninety-nine to find the one. It certainly is an awe-inspiring doubleheader, and fearsome, too. That is, Jesus is fearsome. Everything else trembles before him.

And then he turns toward Jerusalem, turns toward the walled city like a general turning his forces into the hottest part of a battle. A few honest Pharisees (Nicodemus, perhaps?) warn him: "Leave this place and go somewhere else. Herod wants to kill you." Jesus replies, "Go tell that fox, 'I will drive out demons and heal people today and tomorrow, and on the third day I will reach my goal'" (Luke 13:31–32). This man will not be intimidated, will not be deterred. It certainly sets his rebuke of Peter—when he tried to dissuade Jesus—within its context, words that otherwise feel cutting and unnecessarily cruel.

Yes, there is a leisureliness to Jesus. He'll stop whatever he's doing to attend to someone in need. The man never, ever seems to be in a hurry. But his manner can be appreciated only in light of a deeper river flowing in him, this fierce intentionality. Otherwise, you get those popular and ridiculous portraits of Jesus as the wandering storyteller, no more controversial or dangerous than a clerk in a health-food store.

"The life of Jesus went as swift and straight as a thunderbolt," wrote Chesterton, "almost in the manner of a military march; certainly in the manner of the quest of a hero moving to his achievement or his doom."[5] And in the most beautiful turn of events, the hunted becomes the Hunter indeed, as Jesus crucified descends into hell personally, to demand the keys from Satan. What was *that* journey like? Far more than a twilight walk to a cottage. He faces a creature way more terrifying than anything you've met in your nightmares and makes him bend the knee. Then Jesus simply turns and walks back out again, leading a train of rescued captives with him.

Only to race off and catch up with two disciples limping down a road toward a town called Emmaus.

CHAPTER FIVE

THE MOST HUMAN
FACE OF ALL

Now, all of this can begin to sound so lofty and noble that it ends up having an effect *opposite* from the one he intended—we begin to lose Jesus. He's already starting to drift back again heavenward, into the rafters, to take his place in the stained glass.

For something has crept into our assumptions about Jesus that makes it almost impossible to relate to him, not to mention love him. I say "crept" because it has not been a conscious decision; few of the things that shape our actual convictions are. I think much of the creep has happened, ironically, as a result of our attempts to love and revere Christ. But crept in this notion has, and it has done great damage to our perceptions of him, our *experience* of him.

It's the notion that Jesus was really "pretending" when he presented himself as a man.

We who worship Jesus Christ hold fast to the belief that he was God. "Very God of very God," as the Nicene Creed states. The heroic actions and miraculous powers of Jesus' life attest to it. So, when we read what we would call the more human moments, we feel that Jesus was sort of...cheating. With a nod and a wink *we know* that what's *really* happening is that Einstein has dropped in to take the first-grade math quiz. Mozart is playing a measure in the kindergarten song flute choir. After all, we're talking about *Jesus* here. The guy walked on water, raised Lazarus from the dead. He never broke a sweat, right?

But then, what do you make of that terrible sweat in Gethsemane?

They went to a place called Gethsemane, and Jesus said to his disciples, "Sit here while I pray." He took Peter, James and John along with him, and he began to be deeply distressed and troubled. "My soul is overwhelmed with sorrow to the point of death," he said to them. "Stay here and keep watch." Going a little farther, he fell to the ground and prayed that if possible the hour might pass from him. "Abba, Father," he said, "everything is possible for you. Take this cup from me."...And being in anguish, he prayed more earnestly, and his sweat was like drops of blood falling to the ground. (MARK 14:32–36; LUKE 22:44)

Deeply distressed.
Overwhelmed with sorrow.
Anguished.

This doesn't sound like somebody cheating to me. He *begs* his Father, with tears, that this awful cup might be taken from him. Please, let there be some other way. He doesn't want to do it. Sweat like blood pouring from his tormented brow. He pleads with his Father, and then he pleads a second time, and then a third. Does this sound like Einstein adding two and two?

Gethsemane was the most terrible farce if Jesus was faking it.

He was human. Really.

You recall the famous story of his trial in the wilderness? Well, at the end of those forty days of fasting, "he was hungry" (Luke 4:2). On his way into Jerusalem one morning, he goes to have a look at a fig tree, because "he was hungry" (Matt. 21:18). Many readers recall the encounter Jesus had with a woman at a well. The account says that "Jesus, tired as he was from the journey, sat down by the well. It was about the sixth hour. When a Samaritan woman came to draw water, Jesus said to her, 'Will you give me a drink?'" (John 4:6–7). Wait— Jesus was *hungry*? *Tired*? *Thirsty*? Yep. That's what it says. He was human.

The Gospels are filled with beautiful and haunting descriptions of the humanity of Jesus. One of the most poignant takes place when the report reaches him that his cousin John has been guillotined:

> On Herod's birthday the daughter of Herodias danced for them and pleased Herod so much that he promised with an oath to give her whatever she asked. Prompted by her mother, she said, "Give me here on a platter the head of John the Baptist." The king was distressed, but because of his oaths and his dinner guests, he ordered that her request be granted and had John beheaded in the prison. His head was brought in on a platter and given to the girl, who carried it to her mother. John's disciples came and took his body and buried it. Then they went and told Jesus. When Jesus heard what had happened, he withdrew by boat privately to a solitary place. (MATTHEW 14:6–13)

Jesus takes the boat, leaves the crowd behind, and sails to some place he can be alone. The man who has unceasingly offered himself to others needs to get away. He needs room to grieve, just as you would. I cannot say this more emphatically—life *affected* Jesus. "We have spread so many ashes over the historical Jesus that we scarcely feel the glow of His presence anymore," lamented Brennan Manning. "He is a man in a way that we have forgotten men can be: truthful, blunt, emotional, nonmanipulative, sensitive, compassionate."[1]

Jesus never did anything halfheartedly. When he embraced our humanity, he didn't pull a fast one by making a show of it. He embraced it so fully and totally that he was able to die. God can't die. But Jesus did.

It will do your heart good to discover that Jesus shares in your humanity. He was, as the creeds insist, fully human. (Yes, yes—more than that to be sure. But never ever less than that.) I'm sure the chipmunks made him laugh. The Pharisees sure made him furious. He felt joy, weakness, sorrow. The more we can grasp his humanity, the more we will find him someone we can approach, know, love, trust, and adore.

Let me assure you, I cling to the Nicene Creed and the orthodox faith held by the church for ages—Jesus was somehow God and man. A number of ridiculous books have been released in the last hundred years arguing that Jesus was *merely* a man. But a reaction in the other extreme is wrong as well. He is not Mozart playing with the kindergarteners. We're not going to parse here the technicalities theologians have used to try to explain the mechanics of how he became human, yet remained God the Son. To try to dissect that now misses the point. Our little brains seem to be able to hold only one or two thoughts before us anyway. Right now, we are trying to recover his genuine humanity.

Notice how the religious fog even at this moment is working to prevent you: *This is disrespectful. Maybe heresy. He's pushing his point too far. But NOW Jesus is ascended so none of this matters.* The more the dog barks, the closer you are to the bone. Jesus was tired, hungry, thirsty—because he took on our humanity. Read carefully:

The Word became flesh and made his dwelling among us. (JOHN 1:14)

Since the children have flesh and blood, he too shared in their humanity. (HEBREWS 2:14)

When the time came, he set aside the privileges of deity and took on the status of a slave, became *human*! Having become human, he stayed human. It was an incredibly humbling process. He didn't claim special privileges. Instead, he lived a selfless, obedient life and then died a selfless, obedient death—and the worst kind of death at that: a crucifixion. (PHILIPPIANS 2:7–8 The Message)

I mentioned earlier my anger in the museum at the classic art depicting the birth of Jesus the Superbaby. I was angry not because the art was done badly, but because it was done so beautifully, so very reverently, making it all the more difficult to remember that Jesus was *human*. The incarnation is one of the greatest treasures of our faith. The world keeps pushing God away, feeling more comfortable with him up in the heavens somewhere. But in the coming of Jesus he draws near. *Incredibly near.* He takes on our humanity. How could he possibly get closer? He nurses at Mary's breast.

One of my favorite Christmas meditations comes from this passage by Chesterton (he is speaking of Bethlehem, and what it held in its foothills that fateful night):

> The strange kings fade into a far country and the mountains resound no more with the feet of the shepherds; and only the night and the cavern lie in fold upon fold over something more human than humanity.[2]

Savor that passage for a moment. The manger Mary used as a bassinette held something *more* human than humanity? Do you think of Jesus as the most human human-being who ever lived?

It's true.

The ravages of sin, neglect, abuse, and a thousand addictions have left us all a shadow of what we were meant to be. Jesus is humanity in its truest form. His favorite title for himself was the Son of *Man*. Not of God—of man.

We looked to nature and saw reflected there his playfulness, and his fierce intention. Do we see his humanity expressed in creation as well? Well...ummm...look in the mirror. You are the only thing in this world said to be created directly in his image. Your humanity is a reflection of Jesus' humanity. Jesus feels—you feel. Jesus longs—you long. Jesus weeps—you weep. Jesus laughs—you laugh. It's a pretty staggering thought.

Too much "heavens" stuff pushes Jesus away. His humanity brings him close again.

It also helps us recover his captivating personality in the Gospels.

I've always wondered why Jesus, having healed someone, would immediately tell them to keep quiet about it. After giving two blind men perfect vision, "Jesus warned them sternly, 'See that no one knows about this'" (Matt. 9:30). Warned them sternly—now why is that? He does the same after healing a man of leprosy: "Jesus sent him away at once with a strong warning: 'See that you don't tell this to anyone'" (Mark 1:44). A strong warning? But... isn't the point to get the word out? And wouldn't miracles be just the thing? These guys are the poster children now, living proof of Jesus' claims.

Maybe he's using reverse psychology, knowing that the more you insist people don't talk about what happened, the more they will. Is this merely his technique to get the press going? It certainly has that effect. The two blind men "went out and spread the news about him all over that region" (Matt. 9:31). The healed leper "went out and began to talk freely, spreading the news" (Luke 1:45).

But wait—Mark goes on to explain why Jesus did this:

"'See that you don't tell this to anyone. But go, show yourself to the priest and offer the sacrifices that Moses commanded for your cleansing, as a testimony to them.' Instead he went out and began to talk freely, spreading the news. As a result, Jesus could no longer enter a town openly but stayed outside in lonely places. Yet the people still came to him from everywhere" (MARK 1:44–45).

It is a sad editorial footnote. Jesus can't even get a moment's rest now. The paparazzi are everywhere. He doesn't mind a night of prayer on the mountain, but never to be able to get a bed and a hot meal? Jesus' strong warnings reveal his strong *desires*, very human desires. "Please don't tell anybody about this." He doesn't want to be forced to sleep in the woods.

Jesus enjoyed people. Not everyone does, you know. Many stories find him feasting with a rowdy crowd. He invited twelve men to spend day and night with him for three years. His longing for companionship intensifies to a crescendo in Gethsemane: "He took Peter and the two sons of Zebedee along with him.... 'Stay here and keep watch with me'" (Matt. 26:37–38). Don't leave me alone, not now. How urgently human. Yes, Jesus knew loneliness. He's not pretending. The one who created the human heart—whose own heart was so kind and so vast—this man felt deeply. He who created love and friendship longed for it.

Now, there are defenders of the faith—quite vocal in our time, quite convincing in their zeal to protect the glory of God—who will attack you for suggesting that God wants anything from you other than obedience. To suggest so, in their reasoning, is to diminish the all-sufficiency of God. But is that what you see in Gethsemane—a God who couldn't care less whether his friends stay or go? Stay here and keep watch with me. This is no superhero, steeled and impervious to the human condition. Far from it.

And loneliness is something we all share with him. "The whole conviction of my life," wrote Thomas Wolfe, "now rests upon the belief that loneliness, far from being a rare and curious phenomenon, peculiar to myself and to a few other solitary men, is the central and inevitable fact of human existence." To be missed, or misunderstood. To be judged unfairly. To be wanted for what you can do, rather than who you are. To go on for years unappreciated, even unknown by those closest to you. You can hear the pain of being missed in the midst of Jesus' famous words of John 14:

> "Do not let your hearts be troubled. Trust in God; trust also in me. In my Father's house are many rooms; if it were not so, I would have told you. I am going there to prepare a place for you. And if I go and prepare a place for you, I will come back and take you to be with me that you also may be where

I am."...Philip said, "Lord, show us the Father and that will be enough for us." Jesus answered: "Don't you know me, Philip, even after I have been among you such a long time?" (JOHN 14:1–9)

Here, at the very moment Christ is doing all he can to comfort his disciples and prepare them for his coming execution, he not only assures them all will be well, but he promises their companionship will continue for eternity. In this beautiful moment of relational assurance, his closest disciples betray how little they know Jesus, and you can see it hurts him: "Don't you know me...even after I have been among you such a long time?" You can practically see the pain in his eyes.

Imagine living your entire life in a world where the people closest to you don't get you. Oh...you do live in that world. And Jesus understands.

Now, I don't believe that Jesus was always lonely. There are moments of remarkable tenderness recorded in the Gospels. John leaning on his breast at their last supper. Mary washing his feet with tears, wiping them with her hair. I'm sure there were many more. All that time walking the roads with the fellas, all those campfires. I do not believe that his loneliness defined him, as it does many of us. Jesus is an essentially happy man. He loves life. How could the joy of the Lord be our strength if the Lord is seldom joyful?

You might think that keeping Jesus all mysterious and heavenly is the proper thing to do, but consider this: When he came, he came as presented in the Gospels—very much human, a person, a man, with a very distinct personality. This is the primary witness we have of him, recorded for all who would know him. This is how *he* chooses to make himself known. This is the "self" he presents to us. Be careful you don't push him away with your religious delicacies.

"Jesus was so obviously *human*," notes Eugene Peterson, "but this has never been an easy truth for people to swallow. There are always plenty of people walking around who will have none of this particularity: human ordinariness, bodily fluids, raw emotions of anger and disgust, fatigue and loneliness."[3] Perhaps you thought Gethsemane was the only time he sweat? Or maybe we assume his sweat smelled like lilies? And what is with the snowy white robe? Every movie I've seen costumes Jesus in an immaculate white robe. He never got dirty? Those were not paved roads he walked for miles.

You shall know them by their fruit. Jesus' humanity will cause you to fall in love with him all the more. His personality, his remarkable qualities—those we have touched on, those we are about to explore— they burst with color and brilliance like fireworks *because of* his humanity. Think of it—the Man of Sorrows had a sense of humor. The Prince of Peace could work himself into a lather. This wonderful counselor could be downright ironic. The man on a mission had time to sit and chat. Far from diminishing Jesus, this will only quicken your worship and deepen your intimacy.

I love his playfulness. I love his courage. I love his *exasperation*:

To what can I compare this generation? They are like children sitting in the marketplaces and calling out to others: "We played the flute for you, and you did not dance; we sang a dirge, and you did not mourn." For John came neither eating nor drinking, and they say, "He has a demon." The Son of Man came eating and drinking, and they say, "Here is a glutton and a drunkard, a friend of tax collectors and 'sinners.'" (MATTHEW 11:16–19)

He's got to be shaking his head, rolling his eyes. What *is* it with you people? You are simply impossible. John fasted; you thought he was possessed. I feasted; you think I am an alcoholic and a pig. There is simply no pleasing you.

Or how about Jesus' surprise—yes, his genuine surprise (!):

When Jesus had entered Capernaum, a centurion came to him, asking for help. "Lord," he said, "my servant lies at home paralyzed and in terrible suffering." Jesus said to him, "I will go and heal him." The centurion replied, "Lord, I do not deserve to have you come under my roof. But just say the word, and my servant will be healed. For I myself am a man under authority, with soldiers under me. I tell this one, 'Go,' and he goes; and that one, 'Come,' and he comes. I say to my servant, 'Do this,' and he does it." When Jesus heard this, he was astonished and said to those following him, "I tell you the truth, I have not found anyone in Israel with such great faith." (MATTHEW 8:5–10)

Astonished. Variously translated also as "marveled" or "amazed." Matthew uses the exact same word a few paragraphs later to describe the disciples' slack-jawed reaction when Jesus shuts down a storm:

"Lord, save us! We're going to drown!" He replied, "You of little faith, why are you so afraid?" Then he got up and rebuked the winds and the waves, and it was completely calm. The men were amazed and asked, "What kind of man is this? Even the winds and the waves obey him!" (MATTHEW 8:25–27)

Amazed. Astonished. Did you know Jesus could be amazed? Mark uses the word to describe Jesus' amazement at the Jews' unbelief: "He was amazed at their lack of faith" (6:6). The religious glaze over Jesus—or over our hearts—is so thick we have to keep striking it, over and over and over: Jesus was human. Jesus was a man. His humanity was real. He wasn't pretending. Those nails actually hurt.

I can sense the religious trying one more dupe: *Yes, but he's not human now. He's at the right hand of the Father in glory.* The disciples were tempted to think something similar. Late resurrection Sunday, the two fellows from the Emmaus road come rushing back to town to tell the others they have seen Jesus alive. Let's pick up the story there:

> While they were still talking about this, Jesus himself stood among them and said to them, "Peace be with you." They were startled and frightened, thinking they saw a ghost. He said to them, "Why are you troubled, and why do doubts rise in your minds? Look at my hands and my feet. It is I myself! Touch me and see; a ghost does not have flesh and bones, as you see I have." When he had said this, he showed them his hands and feet. And while they still did not believe it because of joy and amazement, he asked them, "Do you have anything here to eat?" They gave him a piece of broiled fish, and he took it and ate it in their presence. (LUKE 24:36–43)

This a very funny moment. The pair from the Emmaus road are in the middle of telling their incredible story when Jesus just appears in the room, as if to illustrate everything they've said. Yep, that was me. Yep, I did it just like that. Suddenly he's just standing there and all he says is, "Peace be with you"?! Here the most fantastic thing in the world is happening before their eyes, and all Jesus says is "Hi"?! His understatement is very, very funny. The disciples are stupefied, dumbfounded; they don't believe that he is real. "Look at my hands and feet." He is clearly showing them the holes the nails pierced. They *still* think he's a ghost. Finally he asks, "Is there anything here to eat?" like a neighbor dropping by for some chips. He chews it carefully in front of them, swallows it, and waits a few seconds for everyone to digest the lesson. You have got to love this moment. *And* the point he's making. Jesus raised is still Jesus, a man—flesh and bones and all. Be gone, religious fog.

Jesus was more human than humanity. His was the most human face of all. This is going to open up wonders for you.

CHAPTER SIX

EXTRAVAGANT
GENEROSITY

I am sitting on the beach this evening, watching the swells roll in toward me. Each wave builds as it approaches, ascending, taking shape, deep greens below sweeping upward into translucent aquamarine. A sculpture in motion, curling forth like shavings from a jade carving. The sheer elegance is enough to take my breath away. The wave I'm fixed upon crashes to the sand like a work of art toppling from its pedestal, but before I can feel the loss another is rushing to take its place, sweeping upward, forward, utterly mesmerizing beauty. Then comes another, then another, and another, in an unending processional.

All things were made through him, comes to mind, *and without him, nothing has been made that has been made*. What are the waves telling us about Jesus?

An artist is revealed in the work he or she creates, and in the *abun-*

dance of the work created. Think of the ocean. Picture it in your mind. Tonight the breakers are thundering on the reef a hundred yards out, and beyond that open ocean. What does this tell us about Jesus? What words come to mind? *Majestic, powerful, wild, dangerous.* Yes, tempestuous, like the clearing of the temple. "His eyes like the grey o' the sea," as Ezra Pound wrote, "the sea that brooks no voyaging." But also gently playful as it laps at your feet, swirling round your toes, pulling the sand away from beneath you as Jesus ever so gently pulls the rug out from under us.

I look down. Scattered at my feet lie a thousand shells, delicate, intricate, the work of a jeweler. An artist with very small tools and exceptional eyesight. If all this is the work of an artist's hand, what does it tell us about the artist? Creation is epic and intimate. *He* is epic and intimate. Everywhere around me, an obsession with beauty and attention to detail.

But most of all, I am thunderstruck by the abundant generosity strewn around, constantly rolling in. It's as if someone took the family silver and ran down the beach, tossing handfuls here and there like a madman. How do you describe this *extravagance*? What kind of person acts like this?

On the third day a wedding took place at Cana in Galilee. Jesus' mother was there, and Jesus and his disciples had also been invited to the wedding. When the wine was gone, Jesus' mother said to him, "They have no more wine." "Dear woman, why do you involve me?" Jesus replied. "My time has not yet come." (JOHN 2:1–4)

Pause—what is his tone of voice at this moment? It makes all the difference. Is he being aloof? Is there a sigh of impatience? Is he irritated? Be careful what you read into the story. His response to Mary seems rude, but that cannot be—we know he adored her. My goodness, while hanging in agony from the cross he arranges for her care. The beauty of their relationship is revealed here as well—she knows all she has to do is ask. There couldn't have been anything condescending in his reply, for she simply turns to the servants and says, like a Jewish mother, "Do whatever he tells you" (v. 5).

> Nearby stood six stone water jars, the kind used by the Jews for ceremonial washing, each holding from twenty to thirty gallons. Jesus said to the servants, "Fill the jars with water"; so they filled them to the brim. Then he told them, "Now draw some out and take it to the master of the banquet." They did so, and the master of the banquet tasted the water that had been turned into wine. He did not realize where it had come from, though the servants who had drawn the water knew. Then he called the bridegroom aside and said, "Everyone brings out the choice wine first and then the cheaper wine after the guests have had too much to drink; but you have saved the best till now." This, the first of his miraculous signs, Jesus performed at Cana in Galilee. He thus revealed his glory, and his disciples put their faith in him. (vv. 6–11)

Wait a second—six stone water jars, holding up to thirty gallons each. That would be somewhere close to 180 *gallons* (John makes the point of saying that the jars were filled "to the brim"). One hundred eighty gallons equals about 682 liters. That would be 908 bottles of wine.

Nine hundred eight.

I know, I know—it seems too extravagant. But the Scripture

makes a point of telling us exactly how many urns there were, how much they held, and even pushes the point that they were filled to the brim. Apparently, the *quantity* Jesus produced is important to the story, and I'm certainly not going to begrudge Jesus the right to be generous.*

John says, "He thus revealed his glory." What is it, exactly, that Jesus thus revealed? Certainly his power over creation. But there is something else here, something beautiful. Jesus did not provide cheap wine—as the maître d' expected, given the lateness of the hour. Nor did he make a statement by substituting grape juice. He didn't just give them a little wine, say, a dozen bottles to wrap up the evening with one last toast. Jesus does it *lavishly*. To the tune of 908 bottles. (Just as the 153 fish the boys "caught" were specifically noted to be *large* fish.) Here is the same stunning generosity we see pouring forth in creation: "The whole earth is filled with his glory" (Isa. 6:3 NLT).

Oh, the beauty of Jesus.

The text declares he hadn't planned on revealing himself at this time—might this help us with our own prayer lives? "Ask and it will be given to you; seek and you will find; knock and the door will be opened to you" (Matt. 7:7)—Jesus would not have urged us to pray if he were unapproachable. Bailing the groom out of an embarrassing situation wasn't Jesus' intention ("my time has not yet come"), but he does it anyway. And not a bit grudgingly. One hundred and eighty

---

* Watch this—if you want proof of the current religious spirit, its ugly nature, watch how folks freak out over this. Websites will crop up. Theologians will step forward to argue the amount ("It says, 'holding from twenty to thirty gallons.'"). Okay, take an average—twenty-five gallons per jar. That's still 150 gallons, 757 bottles. They're not going to like that, so they'll tell you it wasn't really wine, or that their wine isn't like our wine. I'll be accused of encouraging drunkenness. I am not. The Scripture forbids drunkenness. Look—I didn't do the miracle, I just did the math. Are you going to tell Jesus he can't do this?

gallons of top-grade hooch, late into the reception. The crowd has already emptied the cupboards—what is it, close to midnight at this point? This party is going to carry on for hours. What joy, what gladness, how generous and celebratory.

Just like sunshine.

What daily radiance is showered upon us, what immense golden goodness. Every single day, over so much of the planet. It saturates our world, warming the earth, raising the crops in the fields by silent resurrection, unfolding flowers, causing birds to break out in song with the dawning of each day. It bathes everything else in light, which then enables us to behold and enjoy, to live and work and explore. What a gift sunlight is—coming and going. I love getting up in the darkness of early morning and praying through the dawn. As I find myself drawing nearer to God, the room begins to grow lighter and lighter while the spiritual air clears around me. With a final amen, the golden glowing light of sunrise fills the room like the presence of God.

We get hours of it, every day. Hundreds and hundreds of gallons.

And then late afternoon—how beautiful things are when backlit. Autumn grains and grasses, full heads glowing, as if every top were bursting with *shekinah* glory. The gaudy splendor of sunset follows, and then the waiting period of night, to help us appreciate the gift. (Imagine if it were always night, if dawn never came.) But it *does* come, faithfully, lavishly, making our hearts glad once more. What a gift light is! And given in such abundance, we can hardly take it in.

What does sunshine tell us about the personality of Jesus?

What does the gift of our *senses* tell us about Jesus?!

Summer has swept over Colorado. The aspens have fully leaved out after a very wet spring. All the groves are lush, and the breeze in their boughs sometimes sounds like a soft gentle rain shower. When stronger winds blow, it sounds like the surf as it recedes across a pebble beach. What generosity would have created this—bough and leaf and breeze and the human ear just so that we can appreciate the subtleties of its exquisite sounds?

What of touch, the tactile experiences that abound to us? The warmth of riverside stones baked by the sun. We love to hold them after a plunge in the cold water, letting the warmth radiate all the way into our bodies. The comfort of a human caress. And smell—who would have thought of such a thing? The pungent earth after a rain, all creation washed and hung out like the laundry. And hearing—rain on a tin roof, the laughter of your child, music. And *taste*? Watermelon, blue cheese, Tabasco, coffee, chocolate. There is a reason we are warned against gluttony.

What generosity gave us so much? Beauty answers nearly every question.

> Whoever, therefore, is not enlightened
> by such splendor of created things
> is blind;
> whoever is not awakened by such outcries
> is deaf...
> Therefore, open your eyes,
> alert the ears of your spirit, open your lips
> and apply your heart...
> Concerning the mirror of things
> perceived through sensation,
> we can see God...in them, as he is in them.[1]

Now yes, yes, creation sometimes screams a confusing message—fear, pain, grief. Fire burns, rivers flood, winds go hurricane, the earth shudders so hard it levels cities. But you must remember—this was not so in Eden. Mankind fell, surrendering this earth to the evil one. St. Paul says that creation groans for the day of its restoration (see Rom. 8:18–22), making it clear that everything is *not* as it was meant to be. People come to terrible conclusions when they assume this world is exactly as God intended. (An assumption that has wrought havoc in the sciences.) The earth is *broken*.

Which only makes the beauty that *does* flow so generously that much more astounding. And reassuring.

What do we make of the gift of water? You can swim in it, but also float upon it. You can drink it and surf it. Droplets fall from the sky in staggering abundance, yet it also flows in streams and rivers. It makes one sound as a brook, another as a waterfall, and something else altogether in the silence of falling snow. This extravagance is almost scandalous.

Remember—the heart of the artist is revealed in their work. Here and there and everywhere, the creations of Jesus spring like characters from a fairy tale over the earth. Dragonflies? Porcupines? Musk ox, their great shaggy kilts hanging round them and mighty horns swooping down, look like creatures if not from Norse mythology then certainly from ancient times. Not something walking around this moment just north of us. Really now—what do we have here? *Who* do we have here?

You must understand an important distinction—there is Christianity, and then there is church culture. They are not the same. Often they are far from the same. The personality conveyed through much of Christian culture is not the personality of Jesus but of the people in charge of that particular franchise. Tragically, the world looks at funny hats or big hair, gold thrones and purple curtains, stained glass or fog machines and assumes this is what Jesus must be like. When you are confronted with something from Christian culture, ask yourself, *Is this true of the personality of the God of the wind and the desert, the God of sunshine and the open sea?* This will dispel truckloads of religious nonsense. And by beginning his Gospel here, John makes it clear this is quite biblical.

But we were talking about generosity, letting our eyes roam back and forth, as Shakespeare said, "from heaven to earth, from earth to heaven." From the book of nature to the pages of the Gospels:

When he came down from the mountainside, large crowds followed him. A man with leprosy came and knelt before him. (MATTHEW 8:1–2)

When Jesus had entered Capernaum, a centurion came to him, asking for help. (MATTHEW 8:5)

When Jesus came into Peter's house, he saw Peter's mother-in-law lying in bed with a fever. (MATTHEW 8:14)

Two blind men were sitting by the roadside, and when they heard that Jesus was going by, they shouted, "Lord, Son of David, have mercy on us!" (MATTHEW 20:30)

A few days later, when Jesus again entered Capernaum, the people heard that he had come home. So many gathered that there was no room left, not even outside the door. (MARK 2:1–2)

Jesus withdrew with his disciples to the lake, and a large crowd from Galilee followed. (MARK 3:7)

Jesus entered a house, and again a crowd gathered, so that he and his disciples were not even able to eat. (MARK 3:20)

When Jesus got out of the boat, a man with an evil spirit came from the tombs to meet him. (MARK 5:2)

One of the synagogue rulers, named Jairus, came.... Seeing Jesus, he fell at his feet and pleaded earnestly with him, "My little daughter is dying. Please come and put your hands on her so that she will be healed and live." (MARK 5:22–23)

Because so many people were coming and going that they did not even have a chance to eat, he said to them, "Come with me by yourselves to a quiet place and get some rest." So they went away by themselves in a boat to a solitary place. But many who saw them leaving recognized them and ran on foot from all the towns and got there ahead of them. (MARK 6:31–33)

He entered a house and did not want anyone to know it; yet he could not keep his presence secret. In fact, as soon as she heard about him, a woman whose little daughter was possessed by an evil spirit came and fell at his feet. (MARK 7:24–25)

Late into the night, early in the morning, walking down the road, in the middle of his supper, at home, abroad, Jesus offers. His time, his words, his touch, flowing like the wine at Cana. To appreciate the reality of it all, remember, this is not Superman. Remember his loneliness, his weariness, his humanity. This is utterly remarkable—particularly in light of the fact that this is a man on a life-or-death mission. He is lavish with himself.

And that's the key, right there—that giving of himself. That is what is so precious. Moses offered leadership, and tirelessly. Solomon handed out the rarest of wisdom free of charge. Pilot seemed willing to toss to the crowds anyone they wanted. But Jesus gives *himself.* This is, after all, what he came to give, and what we most desperately need.

Jesus points to a field of wheat. Imagine trying to count the number of kernels in one acre. Immeasurable abundance. Turning our gaze to those luxuriant fields, he says, "Listen carefully: Unless a grain of wheat is buried in the ground, dead to the world, it is never any more than a grain of wheat. But if it is buried, it sprouts and reproduces itself many times over" (John 12:24 The Message). The point he is making is that he has come to share his life with us. But again, as soon as I say that, the old religious associations rush in to fog the reality. Imagine walking through a rain forest. Diving over a coral reef. Simply look through a microscope at a drop of pond water. Creation is pulsing with life. It is the life of Jesus, given generously for the life of all things. He is called "the author of life," who personally "sustains all things" (Acts 3:15; Heb. 1:3 NRSV).

This is the life he offers us; this is the extravagance with which he offers it. Jesus doesn't only give his life *for* mankind, he also gives his life *to* mankind. It is showered upon us daily like manna. We'll come back to this in a moment.

For now, we'll simply notice that the man was generous. Extravagant. He still is.

CHAPTER SEVEN

DISRUPTIVE HONESTY

In order to grasp the wildness of this next vignette, I want you to imagine that you have received an invitation to dine at the home of an influential diplomat. The governor or your ambassador will do. A number of dignitaries will be present—bishops of the church, Supreme Court justices, a prime minister. How would your insides feel as you rang the bell? How self-conscious would you be of your appearance, your manners? Alas, thirty seconds after you walk through the door, there is an awkward moment of tension—a delicate matter about forgetting to return the bow of the Dalai Lama. Your host is speechless; you can see from the look on everyone's face that you have committed something a step or two beyond an embarrassing faux pas. What would you say? How would you respond?

When Jesus had finished speaking, a Pharisee invited him to eat with him; so he went in and reclined at the table. But the Pharisee, noticing that Jesus did not first wash before the meal, was surprised. Then the Lord said to him, "Now then, you Pharisees clean the outside of the cup and dish, but inside you are full of greed and wickedness." (LUKE 11:37–39)

Jesus has just entered this man's home, having accepted an invitation to dinner. Every guest who has ever passed through those doors has washed their hands before being seated, slavishly observing a custom unbroken for centuries. It is a test of orthodoxy and solidarity. Jesus knows this, knows they are watching his every move. He walks right past the line at the washbasin and makes himself comfortable at the table. The Pharisee apparently is speechless. Jesus reads the look on his face and offers an explanation: "Oh—the washing bit," he says as he takes a piece of flatbread, breaks a bite off, and chews it. "It completely clouds the issue. Outwardly you look sensational. But inwardly, your heart is full of extortion and evil."

The things Jesus says.

Apparently, he's not concerned about being invited back.

May I remind you that whenever you are watching Jesus, you are watching love. You can always hold that up as you encounter startling passages like this one: "I am at this very moment watching love in action." But...how in the world is this love? It doesn't even seem polite.

Permit me a digression that will help.

Several years ago a beautiful and intelligent young woman whom we love very much began tumbling into a mental breakdown. All those who loved her watched in agony as she became increasingly obsessive, delusional, and depressed. She spiraled downward. We feared for her life. One by one friends and family would make an attempt over coffee or "just dropping by" to bring her back to reality. Her dismissals were offered in such irrational ways we knew she would soon have to be hospitalized. This is a heartbreaking thing to stand by and witness, helplessly, like watching someone fall through the ice.

We arranged what has become known in the mental health community as an "intervention," a gathering of friends and mentors in a united effort to jolt an individual to reality, or, failing that, to insist the person submit to treatment. We began gently. She tossed off our concerns. We became more and more direct. She shifted to self-defense. Finally, we had to be brutally honest and insistent. Even then, she could not grasp the stark reality of her own desperate condition. It was an awkward, painful, and loving thing to do. I'm sorry to say she had to collapse even further before she would accept help.

Jesus' three years of public ministry are one long intervention. That's why he acts the way he does.

Remember, Jesus is not strolling through the Israeli countryside offering poetry readings. He is on a mission to rescue a people who are so utterly deceived most of them don't even *want* to be rescued. His honesty and severity are measured out precisely, according to the amount of delusion and self-deception encasing his listener. When a soul is encrusted with pride, bigotry, self-righteousness, and intellectual elitism—as was his dinner host—then that shell does need to be struck hard at times in order to cause a crack that might allow some light in. Jesus strikes with the precision of Michelangelo.

At another dinner engagement—this one at the home of two now famous sisters—Jesus is pulled into a sibling rivalry:

As they were traveling along, He entered a village; and a woman named Martha welcomed Him into her home. She had a sister called Mary, who was seated at the Lord's feet, listening to His word. But Martha was distracted with all her preparations; and she came up to Him and said, "Lord, do You not care that my sister has left me to do all the serving alone? Then tell her to help me." (LUKE 10:38–40 NASB)

Jesus is a sharp enough man to know not to stick his head in a hornet's nest. These family quarrels have a long tangled history, like Middle Eastern politics. Come to think of it, these quarrels *are* the long tangled history of Middle Eastern politics. Martha demands Jesus take sides. He does, but not as she expected. He takes her side by speaking to what is going on *inside*: "Martha, Martha," the Lord answered, "you are worried and upset about many things, but only one thing is needed. Mary has chosen what is better, and it will not be taken away from her" (vv. 41–42). Jesus is the guest, by the way, in *her* home; *she* made the dinner. If it were me I would have probably tried to diffuse the tension by offering to help Martha myself. Skirt the issue. But that would leave Martha in her self-righteous snit.

I absolutely love the loving courage of this man to say what everyone else knows but won't say.

Jesus' tone seems very different here than with the earlier Pharisee. This is a softer blow; that is because he is dealing with a softer heart. You get the sense that Martha—though snarky at the moment—would be immediately softened by the truthfulness of his words. This is their first reported encounter, but the sisters and their brother Lazarus go on to become close friends of Jesus. Martha's home is his first choice of refuge whenever he is traveling near Jerusalem. Apparently, his disruptive words were just the right touch at just the right moment.

Now, in order to appreciate how beautiful this is, think of how *rarely* it occurs, and how even *more* rarely it is done well. Most people go through their entire lives without anyone, ever, speaking honest, loving, direct words to the most damaging issues in their lives. Pause for a moment, and count the times this has been done for you. Better, pause and count the times you have offered this to someone you love.

We chitchat. We spend our days at a level of conversation as sub-. stantive as smoke. We dance around one another like birds in a mating ritual, bobbing, ducking, puffing out our chests, flapping our wings, circling one another, now advancing, now retreating. If we filmed a week of it in time-lapse photography, it would make the Discovery channel.

Let's be honest—why *aren't* we more honest with each other? Because it will cost us. Socrates didn't exactly get a warm reception for telling the truth. John the Baptist got his head handed to him on a platter for telling it like it is. Kill the messenger. We don't want to pay that bill. If we speak as honestly as Jesus does, if we even *venture* into the hallowed sanctuary of someone else's precious sin, it is going to make the relationship messy to say the least. Why won't you tell your mother-in-law that she is a fearful, controlling woman? Why won't you tell your pastor that his children hate him, hate his sanctified hypocrisy? Why won't you tell your best friend that most of the time they are selfish and self-centered, and you carry all the burden of maintaining the relationship?

We're cowards, that's why.

As I push a little more deeply into my own motives, I realize I just don't care enough. I know what it's like to be with so-and-so. I see their effect on others. But I pretend I don't see; I turn a blind eye. I probably make a dozen choices a day not to see what I see. *We all do.* And why is that, really? Because to risk speaking as Jesus does takes time, because then I'm involved, because who knows what their reaction will be, because, because, because. What I'm saying is I don't really care enough to risk the tension, backlash, penalties, or rejection.

Of course, then it all stays bottled up inside me, fermenting like champagne, so when the cork does pop I speak out of irritation, exasperation, or anger. The tone of which is essentially, "Pull yourself together. Stop making my life so hard." Oh, sure—some people speak "honest words," but their motives are usually despicable.

And so our collective silence—carefully justified as being polite or not wanting to be judgmental or whatever—our silence dooms each of us to remaining that hardened Pharisee or controlling Martha for the rest of our lives. Jesus is the boy in the tale of "The Emperor's New Clothes"—while everyone else fawns and feigns, pretending, looking the other way, he says, "Excuse me, but did you know that you are buck naked?"

What if at this moment you have terminal cancer, but don't know it. The disease is silently ravaging your body while precious days slip by in which you could be taking action. Now—what if your doctor knew, but didn't want to tell you because it would inconvenience him? You'd sue him for malpractice. What if your family knew, but didn't tell you because "they didn't want to upset you"? Or they soften the news of your test results to the point that you don't understand the gravity of your situation. You would be furious.

I'm not stunned by Jesus' words to either of his hosts. I'm stunned by the courage and love this takes.

The man shoots straight. Sometimes he's playful; sometimes he's fierce; the next moment he's generous. This is the beauty of his disruptive honesty—you can count on Jesus to tell you the truth in the best possible way for you to hear it.

One disciple seems ready to enlist: "Teacher, I will follow you wherever you go" (Matt. 8:19). Jesus says the man has no idea what he's signing up for: "Foxes have holes and birds of the air have nests, but the Son of Man has no place to lay his head" (v. 20). The next moment another tries a polite dodge from service: "Lord, first let me go and bury my father" (v. 21). Jesus tells him to climb on board immediately: "Follow me, and let the dead bury their own dead" (v. 22). To Nicodemus—who as a scholar and teacher really shouldn't be so clueless—Jesus says, "You are Israel's teacher...and do you not understand these things?" (John 3:10). The Pharisees claim Abraham. Jesus says, "If you were Abraham's children...then you would do the things Abraham did" (John 8:39). Judas says, "Surely not I, Rabbi?" Jesus answers, "Yes, it is you" (Matt. 26:25).

Jesus is a straight shooter. Sometimes he shoots so straight it practically straightens you out as it passes through you.

Last summer my wife, my friends, and my board of directors urged me to take a sabbatical. A host of issues were involved. Physically, I was exhausted. Dangerously so. There was a nasty stomach problem that couldn't be diagnosed and wouldn't go away. Emotionally, I was angry with people. I'd withdrawn from most of my relationships. I also noticed that I didn't live with much hope; I just threw myself at each day, trying to get on top of things. There was a severity I had long used with myself that had begun to creep into the way I handled others. I read in the Scripture how Jesus was described as praying with "loud cries and tears," and I wondered why I never prayed like that. My prayers felt mechanical. Anyhow, I was in bad shape.

I knew this had to be more than a vacation. The sabbatical would be wasted if I didn't get to the bottom of the issues that caused me to need a sabbatical in the first place. It needed to be open-heart surgery. But my inner world felt like an Oriental rug of issues so intertwined I couldn't sort it out. Early one morning, while I was still lying in bed, looking at the ceiling and asking God to come for me, Jesus asked,

Would you like to know what it is? "Oh, yes, please, Lord," I said. *This is all one thing.* Then a pause for effect. I'm thinking, One thing— this is all just one thing?! *You don't look to me—you look to yourself.*

The truth of it was indisputable the moment Jesus finished speaking. All the years of striving, sacrifice, loneliness, heroic exertion—so much of what I took to be noble about my life was suddenly exposed as godless self-reliance. Utterly godless. I felt naked, like a man lying on an examining table who had just been shown the X-rays of his bone cancer. It was horrifying. And wonderful. Finally, the truth was out.

What would it be like to have someone in your life who knows you intimately, loves you regardless, and is willing to be completely honest with you? Yes, it would be a little unnerving, certainly disruptive— but doesn't part of you also crave it? Most people have to hire this. They pay a therapist to be honest with them because neither their friends nor family have the capacity or willingness to do it well. No matter. Get this however you can.

The more we realize this sort of disruptive honesty is exactly what we need and more difficult to come by than a winning lottery ticket, the more we will fall in love with Jesus for the way he offers it.

Be on your guard against men; they will hand you over to the local councils and flog you in their synagogues. On my account you will be brought before governors and kings as witnesses to them and to the Gentiles. But when they arrest you, do not worry about what to say or how to say it. At that time you will be given what to say, for it will not be you speaking, but the Spirit of your Father speaking through you. Brother will betray brother to death, and a father his child; children will rebel against their parents and have them put to death. All men will hate you because of me, but he who stands firm to the end will be saved. (MATTHEW 10:17–22)

Well this is quite a motivational speech. My goodness, Jesus is sending his boys out for their first solo flight. This is Eisenhower seeing the troops off for D-day. But they get no Henry V at Agincourt inspiration here, no "band of brothers," no Churchill's "finest hour." But maybe this is just what they need to hear. Consider the alternative— what if he told them, "Everything is going to be fine. Just love, and everyone will love you." Then when reality hit and they found themselves bitterly hated and persecuted, they would feel betrayed.

One of the things I most respect about Jesus is his inability to speak nonsense. There is none of that vague Eastern mysticism such as you find in Meng Ke: "A person of great love has no enemies in the world." Jesus Christ proves *that* a ridiculous statement. Or the nihilistic "Practice doing nothing and all will be well" of Lao-Tzu. There are no Ben Franklin colloquialisms, such as "A penny saved is a penny earned." Think of it—what if Jesus was primarily known for saying something like, "Remember to stop and smell the roses"? Proof that you have encountered a distinct *personality* in Jesus is his ability in one tender moment to say the kindest thing and the most startling words the next. What do you make of someone who can lovingly whisper, "Then neither do I condemn you," then shout "Snakes! Reptiles! Sons of hell!"

Now keep in mind, there is a world of difference between being offensive and saying something that offends. It is a matter of *location*— where in fact does the offense lie? The man who makes a racial slur betrays something ugly in him. The friend who says you've had too much to drink spares you something ugly in you. A foghorn is offensive at a dinner party; it is the sweetest sound in the world for a ship lost in a storm. Jesus' words are not offensive. It is something in us that is offended.

We love it when he goes gunning for the Pharisees: "Hypocrites! You travel over land and sea to win a single convert, and when he becomes one, you make him twice as much a son of hell as you are" (Matt. 23:15). Holy cow—did you know Jesus used expressions like "son of hell"? That'd get you kicked out of most churches. But if it weren't for his brutal honesty, we would still be laboring under the weight of all that crushing religious nonsense. If Jesus didn't shoot straight with them, we would be disappointed; it would be hard to respect him. It's when he turns his sights on us that we begin to squirm. And well we should.

Enter through the narrow gate. For wide is the gate and broad is the road that leads to destruction, and many enter through it. But small is the gate and narrow the road that leads to life, and only a few find it. (MATTHEW 7:13–14)

Not everyone who says to me, "Lord, Lord," will enter the kingdom of heaven, but only he who does the will of my Father who is in heaven. Many will say to me on that day, "Lord, Lord, did we not prophesy in your name, and in your name drive out demons and perform many miracles?" Then I will tell them plainly, "I never knew you. Away from me, you evildoers!" (MATTHEW 7:21–23)

I am the way and the truth and the life. No one comes to the Father except through me. (JOHN 14:6)

This is, without question, the Great Offense of Jesus Christ—his exclusivity.

To make sure we understand this, what he is saying is that he alone is the means to heaven. No one comes to the one true God except through him.

Offensive as the claim may be, we still have to deal with it. Either it is arrogant, or it is true.

No other leader of the world's religions makes such an audacious claim. It is a line in the sand that has caused many Christians embarrassment (particularly those trying to win acceptance in our "all roads lead to Rome" postmodern world). F. F. Bruce wrote a helpful book titled *Hard Sayings of Jesus*, in which he tackled many of the canon shots fired off by Christ—plucking out your eye, pearls before swine—but I am sorry to report he did not address these claims, which are clearly the hardest of all.

Now yes, yes, I understand that many men have used these statements in a spirit quite apart from the spirit of Christ. Yes, many times it seems as though those who preach on hellfire wish you would go there. But that fact has no bearing whatsoever on the actual *existence* of hellfires. If they do exist, it would be demented evil not to warn you. Waaay beyond malpractice. The religious spirit has used the question of hell to distort left and right, so it would be good to pause and clarify what the heart of God is on these matters:

> The Lord is not slow in keeping his promise, as some understand slowness. He is patient with you, not wanting anyone to perish, but everyone to come to repentance. (2 PETER 3:9)

Not wanting any to perish. God does not want to lose a single human soul. In fact, those hellfires weren't even created for man.

They were created for the devil and his demons (Matthew 25:41). Jesus isn't secretly hoping that you'll go there. Listen to his lament over his own stubborn people:

O Jerusalem, Jerusalem, you who kill the prophets and stone those sent to you, how often I have longed to gather your children together, as a hen gathers her chicks under her wings, but you were not willing! (LUKE 13:34)

Jesus' heart of love is not diminished by the fact that some people will actually choose hell over surrendering to God. He weeps over it. He warns, urges, pleads, performs miracles. As they nail him to the timbers, he says, "Father, forgive them, for they do not know what they are doing" (Luke 23:34). Because if they *don't* find forgiveness, it is going to be a mighty black day of reckoning. Jesus prays for them, prays they will find mercy.

Most attempts to convince the world that Jesus was a "really great guy, not mean and dogmatic like You-Know-Who" (usually meaning Republicans and the Religious Right) carry their task all the way to the point of hiding or eliminating the exclusivity of Jesus. "Well, yes, but he didn't *mean* all that. These are doctrines added later by the church." Practically the opposite is true—Jesus said it very clearly. It is the church who has often tried to explain it away.

Thomas Jefferson couldn't bring himself to believe the miracles of Jesus; he felt they were an embarrassment to his otherwise profound ethical teaching. So he took a kitchen knife and cut those passages out of his personal Bible. Many folks do the same when it comes to Jesus' exclusive claims. But Jesus made those claims, every one of them, just as surely as he did those miracles. The church has held it to be a matter of orthodoxy since its creation at Pentecost.

I don't know that we fully appreciate what a gift it is to have someone so immovable.

We take our relativism casually, where and when we find it convenient. "Cream and sugar? Sexual preference? Universalism?" But what if everything *was* relative—including reality itself? Remember your last nightmare—remember what a relief it was to wake and find you had been dreaming? To come out of a night terror is one of the most profound reliefs common to humankind. Sitting bolt upright with a gasp or a scream, you discover that you are safe in your own bed. Your whole body relaxes, your breathing slows, your whirling brain cools down. You have been "saved," so to speak, by reality.

Now—imagine what it would be like if you were never, ever able to wake from your nightmares. Like being tumbled under the waves and never able to find the surface again. There are many poor souls living out such torment in our mental institutions. Those who have overdosed on drugs can tell you how horrifying this is. One night, many years ago, a friend and I took five times the amount of hallucinogens then being used by recreational drug idiots. I thought I would never climb out of it. When I woke on a stinking cot in a jail cell, I was utterly overjoyed. That there *is* a reality for us to wake to is a gift beyond words.

Whether or not we choose to face that reality is quite up to us.

Truth or reality is avoided when it is painful. We can revise our maps only when we have the discipline to overcome that pain. To have such discipline, we must be totally dedicated to truth. That is to say we must always hold truth, as best we can determine it, to be more important, more vital to our self-interest, than our comfort. Conversely, we must always consider our personal discomfort relatively unimportant and, indeed, even welcome it in the service of the search for truth. Mental health is an ongoing process of dedication to reality at all costs.[1]

Thus the startling, disruptive, sometimes brutal honesty of Jesus. The world is stone drunk, and raging at Jesus because he's trying to keep us from taking the car. Who is being unreasonable?

The spirit of our day is a soft acceptance of everything—except deep conviction in anything. This is where Jesus will suddenly confront the world as a great rock confronts the river flowing ever downhill. He is immovable. The cry used to be for "tolerance," by which we meant, "We have very strong differences, but we will not let those be the cause of hatred or violence between us." Now it is something else, where all convictions are softened to second or third place while we all agree to enjoy the world as much as we can. But truth is not like conviction. Conviction might be a matter of personal opinion, but truth is like a great mountain, solid and immovable whether we like it or even acknowledge it. Christianity is not a set of convictions—it is a truth. The most offensive thing imaginable.

Jesus is a rock, all right. "A stone of stumbling and a rock of offense" (Rom. 9:33 NASB). A rock is offensive in your shoe, because it is an inconvenience. If we said, "Away with all rocks!" we would wish the planet right out from under our feet. But a rock is also the only refuge from the raging seas. The shipwrecked soul doesn't curse the rock because it is immovable; he clings to it, weeping for gratitude.

Remember—when Jesus tells us the truth, he doesn't say, "You are on your own now. Deal with it." He offers us a way out. As John said, "For the law was given through Moses; grace and truth came through

Jesus Christ" (1:17). Truth *and* grace. Anytime, every time Jesus pulls the rug out from under us, he extends his hand to lift us to a place of refuge.

Sometimes those he reaches his hand to are so far out of the mainstream it is scandalizing.

CHAPTER EIGHT

A SCANDALOUS FREEDOM

Early on in the fanfare of his public appearances, Jesus gives what will become known as the famous Sermon on the Mount. This is a "big moment" for Jesus. He has laid out in detail his understanding of a life that pleases God; he has, so to speak, driven a stake in the ground. His star is ascending, crowds are growing, and the religious leaders are watching his every move. Watch what Jesus does next:

> Large crowds followed Jesus as he came down the mountainside. Suddenly, a man with leprosy approached him and knelt before him. "Lord," the man said, "if you are willing, you can heal me and make me clean." Jesus reached out and touched him. "I am willing," he said. "Be healed!" And instantly the leprosy disappeared. (MATTHEW 8:1–3 NLT)

It sounds like a very nice Bible story—until you understand what Jesus has done. First, this leprosy thing. Few of us have met a "leper." The word has since become hijacked by the religious haze; we hardly have a reaction to it other than, "poor guy." Substitute AIDS. Think of the public attitude, especially early in the AIDS crisis, when people were afraid to go to their dentist for fear of catching it somehow. Picture this man as someone in the late stages of AIDS—emaciated body, nearly bald, wheezing, face ravaged by ulcers.

Second, the Jewish attitude toward those infected. Lepers were required to cry out as they passed through a village, "Unclean! Unclean!" warning their neighbors lest unwitting citizens accidently touch them—and become religiously defiled themselves. Leviticus 13:45–46 made it clear that "the person with such an infectious disease must wear torn clothes, let his hair be unkempt, cover the lower part of his face, and cry out 'Unclean! Unclean!' As long as he has the infection he remains unclean. He must live alone; he must live outside the camp." Clothed in rags, bandanna over the face, hair dirty and matted. Talk about ostracism. In Israel at that time, to get within a stone's throw of someone so diseased was to jeopardize your own righteousness and reputation.

So, that is the danger Jesus is faced with. The man comes near Jesus—but not too near. What does Jesus do?

He reaches out and touches him.

The beauty of this is beyond words.

Jesus doesn't need to come in contact with the man in order to heal him. There are many accounts where all he does is say the word and people are healed, even people a county away. Yet he *touches* him. Why?! Mark's version of the story says that Jesus was "moved with compassion" (1:41 NASB). He who can be so immovable is actually moved rather easily, moved for all the right reasons. Because this is the one thing the man needs. No one has touched him for a very long time. To be starved for human touch is far worse than to starve for bread. The kindness of Jesus in this one act is enough to make me fall in love with him.

But so is his scandalous freedom.

Because now, Jesus is defiled. At least, in the eyes of all the proper authorities he is.

Jesus is just getting his ministry going. He has a message he needs to get across, for by his own admission, "That is why I have come" (Mark 1:38). Credibility is fairly important at this point—especially given the fact that in this recent tour de force of a sermon, he has begun to challenge cherished notions of the pontifical tyrants. But here, in his very next move, Jesus is almost guaranteeing he will be disqualified. Emotionally, *politically*, this would be the social equivalent of a rising priest or pastor giving their most important message of the year, then stepping outside onto the front porch of the church, lighting a cigarette, and taking a good long shot of tequila straight from the bottle as the congregation files past. Metaphorically speaking.

Jesus doesn't seem to care.

Or better, he cares very deeply *about the right things*.

He knows exactly what he's doing. In the Sermon on the Mount he completely overhauled their understanding of goodness. In a sort of moral Copernican revolution, he moves the concept of righteousness from the external to the internal. It is a far, far more demanding holiness, but one that will overturn legalism like a fruit cart. And then, almost as if to say, "Let me show you what I mean," we have this story.

The risks Jesus is willing to take with his reputation are simply stunning.

To give this a proper church contrast, permit me to recount a conversation from a staff meeting held at a church I worked for many years ago. The several pastors on the payroll assembled each week to hear our directives from the senior pastor. This particular week he chose alcohol as his topic. The verse he read was from the book of Romans: "It is better not to eat meat or drink wine or to do anything else that will cause your brother to fall" (14:21). Then followed his application: "So, we don't want to be seen out there in a restaurant ordering alcohol. You don't want to make a member of our congregation stumble now, do you?" "What about in our homes?" one of the bold (and short-termed) assistant pastors inquired. "Are you comfortable with that?" "Someone from the congregation might drop by anytime, unannounced." "What if we keep our curtains drawn?" You see the ridiculous downward spiral of the conversation. After leading us oh so reverently to the *reductio ad absurdum*—sneaking a sip of cabernet late at night with the lights off and curtains drawn—he then concluded for us: "It would be a sin to drink as a member of this pastoral team."

I wanted to raise my hand and ask if—knowing how many more people in our culture struggle with their weight—the principle applied to eating in public as well. I bit my tongue. But it is just this sort of religious rule-making that takes us right back to the Levitical law. This is the very line of reasoning used to take away the freedom of New Testament Christianity and exchange it for the shackles of a slave, wrapping honest Christians in more chains than Marley's ghost. Down through the ages, the religious have filled the church with this sort of justified legalism.

Returning to the risks Jesus is willing to take, behold his utter freedom in the famous story of "the woman at the well."

[Jesus] left Judea and went back once more to Galilee. Now he had to go through Samaria. So he came to a town in Samaria

called Sychar, near the plot of ground Jacob had given to his son
Joseph. Jacob's well was there, and Jesus, tired as he was from
the journey, sat down by the well. It was about the sixth hour.
When a Samaritan woman came to draw water, Jesus said to
her, "Will you give me a drink?" (His disciples had gone into
the town to buy food.) The Samaritan woman said to him,
"You are a Jew and I am a Samaritan woman. How can you ask
me for a drink?" (For Jews do not associate with Samaritans.)
(JOHN 4:3–9)

Slow down, slow down. Our familiarity with these stories numbs
us. What do we have here? Jews despise Samaritans; they don't *ever*
speak to them. As Paul Johnson points out, "The Samaritans were
hated by the Jews... [with] a quasi-religious fury and a form of local
racism of the most ferocious temper."[1] Insert the attitude of Southern
whites in the Klan toward blacks in the 1920s. Furthermore, a Jewish
man would never speak to a Jewish woman; a rabbi would *never ever*
speak to a Samaritan woman. One more detail—this woman is sexually loose. She has what used to be called a "reputation." She is sexually indiscreet at a time that wantonness could get a girl stoned.

So, we have a single Jewish man and a single Samaritan woman
meeting at a well. Alone. Against every convention, the man initiates
a conversation. What is the girl to think? She's had more than a few
drinks bought for her in the past. This encounter is scandalous right
from the start. This is a white man asking a black woman for a ride in
her car in Birmingham at the height of segregation. Jesus doesn't even
hesitate; he is utterly free from those religious and social prejudices
disguised as "What good people do." He is willing to take what would
have been considered fatal risks with his reputation. We'll come back
to this story in a minute.

Meanwhile, it is with regard to the religious that Jesus seems most radically free. His attitude toward the Sabbath is shocking:

> At that time Jesus went through the grain fields on the Sabbath. His disciples were hungry and began to pick some heads of grain and eat them. When the Pharisees saw this, they said to him, "Look! Your disciples are doing what is unlawful on the Sabbath." He answered, "Haven't you read what David did when he and his companions were hungry? He entered the house of God, and he and his companions ate the consecrated bread—which was not lawful for them to do, but only for the priests. Or haven't you read in the Law that on the Sabbath the priests in the temple desecrate the day and yet are innocent? I tell you that one greater than the temple is here. If you had known what these words mean, 'I desire mercy, not sacrifice,' you would not have condemned the innocent. For the Son of Man is Lord of the Sabbath." (MATTHEW 12:1–8)

Jesus' students, his soon-to-be-ambassadors, are flagrantly breaking the Sabbath. Jesus defends them. You understand that by this point, the authorities think he is far too dangerous. And he is. In their minds, he is continually breaking the law and encouraging others to do so. They see him as an outlaw; they certainly end up hanging him like one.

In order to understand what compels this man, you must keep in mind the distinction between the laws of God and the laws of men, and furthermore, that magnificent difference between the spirit of the law and the letter of the law.

Allow me another contrast for clarity. A dear friend attended a Christian college. Part of their agreement required students to attend chapel three times weekly. In addition to this, freshmen were required to join one of many midweek campus Bible studies; they were also "strongly encouraged" to "become an active member" in a local church. This would amount to five religious gatherings per week at a minimum—for students who were already in a far richer daily Christian community than 99 percent of churchgoers, and also under daily discipleship from Christian teachers.

Now, a word on the Sabbath. When it was established by God in Genesis chapter 2, it was clearly for rest: "By the seventh day God had finished the work he had been doing; so on the seventh day he rested from all his work. And God blessed the seventh day and made it holy, because on it he rested from all the work of creating that he had done" (vv. 2–3). The Jews understood this well. No work was allowed on the Sabbath. "Six days you shall labor, but on the seventh day you shall rest; even during the plowing season and harvest you must rest" (Exod. 34:21). You must rest.

Furthermore, Jesus makes clear that the Sabbath was made for man, not the other way around. In other words, we don't serve the Sabbath—the Sabbath serves *us*. My friend chose not to attend church on Sundays. This was met with frowns and suspicion; he was dismissed as a marginally committed Christian. This is ridiculous; religious activity drunkenness, gluttony. These students were overloaded with extraordinary demands of study. Daily homework was a millstone hung round their necks, requiring them to labor way into the hours of every night. Sleep deprivation was standard on campus. If anyone needed a day of rest come Sunday, it was these beleaguered disciples. Rather than lifting the workload on Sunday, the college culture added yet one more duty. Thus violating the spirit of the law, while pretending to honor it.

This is a very mild example of how suffocating religious institutions can become.

But they always have their reasons; the leaders of this college will fight for the policies they have created. There is an old joke about why Baptists don't make love standing up—because people might think they're dancing. It captures the absurdity of legalism beautifully. This measly, picayune, trivial, petty rule-making actually ends up hardening your heart to God while stiffening your self-righteousness. No wonder Jesus hates this stuff.

Some Pharisees and teachers of the law came to Jesus from Jerusalem and asked, "Why do your disciples break the tradition of the elders? They don't wash their hands before they eat!" [Jesus replied,] "You hypocrites! Isaiah was right when he prophesied about you: 'These people honor me with their lips, but their hearts are far from me. They worship me in vain; their teachings are but rules taught by men.'" Jesus called the crowd to him and said, "Listen and understand. What goes into a man's mouth does not make him 'unclean,' but what comes out of his mouth, that is what makes him 'unclean.'" Then the disciples came to him and asked, "Do you know that the Pharisees were offended when they heard this?" He replied, "Every plant that my heavenly Father has not planted will be pulled up by the roots. Leave them; they are blind guides. If a blind man leads a blind man, both will fall into a pit." Peter said, "Explain the parable to us."

"Are you still so dull?" Jesus asked them. "Don't you see that whatever enters the mouth goes into the stomach and then out of the body? But the things that come out of the mouth come from the heart, and these make a man 'unclean.' For out of the heart come evil thoughts, murder, adultery, sexual immorality, theft, false testimony, slander. These are what make a man 'unclean'; but eating with unwashed hands does not make him 'unclean.'" (MATTHEW 15:1–2, 7–20)

You can hear his disgust. Hypocrites. Blind guides. Then, as with the Sermon on the Mount, Jesus sets before us a deeper, *truer* view of holiness. The issues are first and foremost internal, before they are ever external. You can murder someone without ever pulling a trigger. You break the Sabbath if come Sunday night you're exhausted. Especially if you've been exhausted by church. Letter, and spirit. All those external "rules of men" do nothing to promote a genuine holiness. But they do make people Pharisees. By the truckload.

Jesus' freedom is a difficult thing to teach on for many reasons; let me name two. First, there are certain types who will hear this and find it an excuse to live as they please. Many characters in our irreverent age "don't care what others think." Their freedom is abrasive and unholy. The freedom Jesus models is not a crass "giving the finger to the world." Or the church, for that matter.

Others will dismiss the freedom Jesus offers out of fear—either the fear of what people might think (which, ironically, is sin), or the fear of "falling into immorality." So let me be very clear—the scandalous freedom Jesus models for us is based in an understanding of a holiness much deeper than anything the religious ever concocted. Remember, "Unless your righteousness surpasses that of the Pharisees and the teachers of the law, you will certainly not enter the kingdom of heaven" (Matt. 5:20). The only possible way that can happen is through an internal revolution, a changed heart. When we have a heart like Jesus'.

One more example:

One of the Pharisees invited Jesus to have dinner with him, so he went to the Pharisee's house and reclined at the table. When a woman who had lived a sinful life in that town learned that Jesus was eating at the Pharisee's house, she brought an alabaster jar of perfume, and as she stood behind him at his feet weeping, she began to wet his feet with her tears. Then she wiped them with her hair, kissed them and poured perfume on them. (LUKE 7:36–38)

Whoa. Here is yet another scandalous scene. This "fallen woman" is wiping Jesus' feet with her hair, and *kissing* them. A very intimate encounter. She obviously has lost her capacity to care what the "nice people" think, and Jesus doesn't seem to have ever bothered trying that capacity on. He is no "respecter of persons." Not, at least, as it is with most folks in this world, *especially* leaders. This is utterly remarkable in the society of the religious, for the fear of man rules that world. "What good people might think" is a very, very powerful motivator and the raison d'être for most of the ridiculous policies.

When the Pharisee who had invited him saw this, he said to himself, "If this man were a prophet, he would know who is touching him and what kind of woman she is—that she is a sinner." (v. 39)

Can you believe the arrogant self-righteousness of these guys? It is a sinner who invited him to dinner. It is a sinner who is running the synagogue, too. Jesus answers patiently this time—apparently, this Pharisee is open to a new way of understanding goodness.

Jesus answered him, "Simon, I have something to tell you." "Tell me, teacher," he said. "Two men owed money to a certain moneylender. One owed him five hundred denarii, and the other fifty. Neither of them had the money to pay him back, so he canceled the debts of both. Now which of them will love him more?" Simon replied, "I suppose the one who had the bigger debt canceled." "You have judged correctly," Jesus said. (vv. 39–43)

Having rescued Simon from the religious spirit, Jesus turns to attend to the precious heart of this brave woman who has entered so boldly, so humbly. She is exposed to the scornful stares of the other guests; they are whispering loudly. Jesus covers her:

Then he turned toward the woman and said to Simon, "Do you see this woman? I came into your house. You did not give me any water for my feet, but she wet my feet with her tears and wiped them with her hair. You did not give me a kiss, but this woman, from the time I entered, has not stopped kissing my feet. You did not put oil on my head, but she has poured perfume on my feet. Therefore, I tell you, her many sins have been forgiven—for she loved much. But he who has been forgiven little loves little." Then Jesus said to her, "Your sins are forgiven." The other guests began to say among themselves, "Who is this who even forgives sins?" Jesus said to the woman, "Your faith has saved you; go in peace." (LUKE 7:44–50)

If you don't understand this scene, you won't understand Christian holiness. If you don't find this one of the most beautiful stories you have ever read, you won't *want* Christian holiness. And you sure won't understand Jesus.

The man is free—free from what people think, free from religion, free from false obligation. People won't like it, won't understand it;

they'll draw false conclusions, point fingers, and worse. He is free from that as well. Oh to be so free.

The more you fall in love with Jesus' genuine goodness, which is true goodness, the more you will absolutely detest the counterfeit of a false piety and a shallow morality. As he did. Jesus has a wild freedom *born out of a profound holiness.*

Which makes him the most remarkable person I have ever known.

To do them justice, the people who crucified Jesus did not do so because he was a bore. Quite the contrary; he was too dynamic to be safe. It has been left for later generations to muffle up that shattering personality and surround him with an atmosphere of tedium.[2]

CHAPTER NINE

CUNNING

In a piece of advice that could have been lifted from a CIA training manual or the whispered meetings of a revolutionary cell, Jesus tells his little platoon, "I am sending you out like sheep among wolves. Therefore be as shrewd as snakes and as innocent as doves" (Matt. 10:16). We like the innocent as doves part; that sounds nice. Very Sunday school. But that first bit—hold on now. Shrewd as *snakes*? When you hear someone say, "He's such a snake," do you think, *Oh—what a fine Christian*?

The things Jesus says.

Let's get the religious drapery off this. A dove and a snake. Surely they remember the dove descending on Jesus. As for the snake metaphor—these Jews would have connected that instantly to the serpent in the Garden. Be as holy as the Spirit and be as cunning as

Satan. You want us to do *what*?! Jesus is saying, "Look, this is a very dangerous world." The disciples glance at one another, thinking, *Right. We've got the Son of God on our side.* "I mean it," he continues. "Take this seriously. I'm sending you into the Congo with a butter knife. You are easy pickings. You must be holy and you *must* be cunning."

They've been watching Jesus for a few years now. His way of maneuvering must have given this command a sober weightiness.

Let's go back and pick up our earlier clarity (probably lost by now) regarding the *context* of Jesus' life—those murdered little boys, their parents wailing, the angel in the night, Jesus bundled tight beneath a cloak as his parents fled the country. Jesus is a hunted man. Many times over these past three years he has ducked out of town because the thugs were waiting to take him. He is no fool. He knows full well he is operating behind enemy lines. Oh, he intends a revolution, but he knows timing is essential. He must outwit his enemy, circumvent the religious authorities without seeming to do so, and train his followers to carry on after his departure—despite the fact they appear to have the common sense of a three-year-old.

Now watch him navigate.

Shortly after the temptation in the wilderness, Jesus is performing miracles, casting out demons. He has drawn to himself the outcast. The crowds begin to swell with the downtrodden; the air is electric with the thrill of something new. Something smacking of revolt. The mob will soon try to seize Jesus and make him king by force (he ducks out of that scene, as well, and relocates). So he offers this:

> Do not think that I have come to abolish the Law or the Prophets; I have not come to abolish them but to fulfill them. I tell you the truth, until heaven and earth disappear, not the smallest letter, not the least stroke of a pen, will by any means disap-

pear from the Law until everything is accomplished. Anyone who breaks one of the least of these commandments and teaches others to do the same will be called least in the kingdom of heaven, but whoever practices and teaches these commands will be called great in the kingdom of heaven. (MATTHEW 5:17–19)

Over the course of the next few years, Jesus' movement will disrupt the Jewish system very, very profoundly. He is going to turn things upside down and inside out. The world will never be the same. Literally. But there is a precision to his every move. Without his teaching on genuine holiness, the crowd could shift to anarchy. Mob psychology is stable as plutonium. One crowd tried to throw him off a cliff already. Another will try a coup. Don't forget—this is the age of the coliseums.

And he's got to keep the religious authorities off-balance as well. "I've not come to abolish the law, not the smallest letter, not the least stroke of a pen....Anyone who breaks one of the least of these commandments and teaches others to do so will be called least in the kingdom of heaven." He's got the mob suddenly thinking about their morals and the religious police stumped as to his intentions. Brilliant.

Now, the conflict is going to escalate. But still, Jesus will not be suckered in prematurely. He continues to maneuver:

Then the Pharisees went out and laid plans to trap him in his words. They sent their disciples to him along with the Herodians. "Teacher," they said, "we know you are a man of integrity and that you teach the way of God in accordance with the truth. You aren't swayed by men, because you pay no attention to who they are. Tell us then, what is your opinion? Is it right to pay taxes to Caesar or not?" But Jesus, knowing their evil intent, said, "You hypocrites, why are you trying to trap me? Show me the coin used for paying the tax." They brought him a denarius, and he asked them, "Whose portrait is this? And whose inscription?" "Caesar's," they replied. Then he said to them, "Give to Caesar what is Caesar's, and to God what is God's." When they heard this, they were amazed. So they left him and went away. (MATTHEW 22:15–22)

He will not be baited into their traps; he will not be sidelined as a member of "this group" or "that position." Guilt by association is an easy trump card in public life. If you can label your opponent as Right Wing or Liberal, Fundamentalist or Charismatic, you don't even have to argue your case. Your fellow partisans will dismiss the culprit with righteous indignation. Branding someone prevents them from ever being able to prove they are innocent, state their case. It's a cheap and effective ploy that's been around a long time, a particular favorite of the religious. Tar and feather 'em.

Jesus won't be tricked into it. He circumvents the Roman loyalists and anyone looking for a reason to report him to Caesar by saying, "Give him what is his." He keeps himself firmly established as a good Jew by adding, "And give God what is his." Brilliant. Have you taken notice of how *smart* Jesus is? And cunning as a snake.

"By what authority are you doing these things?" they asked. "And who gave you this authority?" Jesus replied, "I will also ask you one question. If you answer me, I will tell you by what authority I am doing these things. John's baptism—where did it come from? Was it from heaven, or from men?" They discussed it among themselves and said, "If we say, 'From heaven,' he will ask, 'Then why didn't you believe him?' But if we say,

'From men'—we are afraid of the people, for they all hold that John was a prophet." So they answered Jesus, "We don't know." Then he said, "Neither will I tell you by what authority I am doing these things." (MATTHEW 21:23–27)

The clerical stooges dare to question his authority. He turns the trial on them so completely they find themselves backed into the corner they had hoped to box him into. Now they don't know what to say or do. Jesus says, "If you won't answer me, I don't have to answer you." Then he just walks away. Beautiful.

But the best use Jesus makes of his cunning brilliance is with the hearts he is trying to win over. This is a far more difficult task. Let's return to the story of the woman at the well; we left it too soon. There is so much more there worth relishing. Remember now—single Jewish man, single Samaritan woman. She is sexually indiscreet. They are alone. He strikes up a conversation. *She* knows it's scandalous—"You're a Jew. I'm a Samaritan woman." She adds "woman" to make the point. "How is it you ask me for a drink?" Exactly. What's a girl supposed to read into this?

She's a tough cookie, this one. A more submissive first-century Palestinian woman with no legal rights would have just drawn the water and not said a word, whatever she might have been thinking. But this one, she puts up a fight. I already like her. Jesus replies,

If you knew the gift of God and who it is that asks you for a drink, you would have asked him and he would have given you living water. (JOHN 4:10)

A return that almost implies, "Hold your horses there, cowgirl— you don't know what you're getting yourself into." Her rebuttal is feisty:

"Sir," the woman said, "you have nothing to draw with and the well is deep. Where can you get this living water?" (v. 11)

You can almost see her—one hand on a hip, jug in the other, head cocked in that sassy way. "Where you gonna get water? You got no rope," and you can sense the insinuated "You got no rope, *Rabbi.*" Then she tosses in a bit of the racial tension:

Are you greater than our father Jacob, who gave us the well and drank from it himself, as did also his sons and his flocks and herds? (v. 12)

Samaritans were hated because they were half-breeds. Dragging Jacob into this is a defiant, "Do you think you're better than me?" A comment that would have incensed your average Pharisee. She's picking a fight. The repartee here is worth the entire account. But wait, there's more—Jesus doesn't take the bait. His next comment is pure intrigue:

"Everyone who drinks this water will be thirsty again, but whoever drinks the water I give him will never thirst. Indeed, the water I give him will become in him a spring of water welling up to eternal life." The woman said to him, "Sir, give me this water so that I won't get thirsty and have to keep coming here to draw water." He told her, "Go, call your husband and come back." "I have no husband," she replied. (vv. 13–17)

Jesus is setting a trap. She throws one verbal jab after another, like a waitress in a rough cantina. He has the deftness of a bullfighter. She's snarky, then defensive; he's gracious and engaging. Then something in her attitude seems to shift—notice the piece of critical information she chooses to *hide*: "I'm not married." Technically, that's true. Anything else? She *is* living with a man—why doesn't she admit that? "I'm not seeing anyone right now." Is she coming on to Jesus a little bit, this winsome man who has continued to pursue her, alone, outside of town? Something provokes him to say, "Go get your husband."

Now he has her right where he wants her, and he pulls the chair out from under her:

You are right when you say you have no husband. The fact is, you have had five husbands, and the man you now have is not your husband. What you have just said is quite true. (vv. 17–18)

Snap. He's got her.

To appreciate his style, consider it would have been a lot easier for Jesus to go about the whole conversation in a more direct manner: "Hello, I'm the Messiah. What's your name?" "Hello, I notice you're here midday. Is that because you are on your sixth relationship?" As he so often does, Jesus takes the *indirect approach*. Playful, and cunning. Very cunning. I would love to know how long that pause was, see the look on her face after he reads her the secrets of her diaries. Does she drop her bucket?

And notice—he doesn't throw the seventh command at her. He simply tells her that he knows what she's hiding. Most embarrassing. She actually tries one more racial/religious card, maybe to deflect the attention off her. Jesus holds his ground. He must be smiling at her now, because she doesn't fight back after that. "I know that Messiah...is coming. When he comes, he will explain everything to us" (v. 25). This is the humblest thing she has said yet. Essentially, she's asking, "Are you who I *think* you are?!" Jesus simply says, "Yep." What a wonderful way of capturing this woman. The story ends with her running to tell the whole village, and in generous Jesus fashion, he stays two days with them. A Jewish rabbi hanging out with the Samaritans.

To get the full texture and zest of his cunning in these stories, weave together his playfulness with his honesty, his generosity with his fierce intention. Add a dash of his startling freedom. I love this man.

Now watch him with "the rich young ruler":

As Jesus started on his way, a man ran up to him and fell on his knees before him. "Good teacher," he asked, "what must I do to inherit eternal life?" (MARK 10:17)

Jesus is starting out of town. In order to fall on his knees before him, this fellow would have to have blocked his way. One last interruption throws himself in front of Jesus with just a little drama. Jesus acts as though this is just one more religious type, feigning flattery but entrenched in their holier-than-thou self-assessment.

"Why do you call me good?" Jesus answered. "No one is good—except God alone. You know the commandments: 'Do not murder, do not commit adultery, do not steal, do not give false testimony, do not defraud, honor your father and mother.'" (vv. 18–19)

Don't flatter me. You know the commands—keep them. He tosses him a standard Jewish answer, a reply that seems like an end to the conversation because he apparently turns to walk away. The sincerity of the man then becomes apparent:

"Teacher," he declared, "all these I have kept since I was a boy." Jesus looked at him and loved him. (vv. 20–21)

"Teacher," in order to stop Jesus, then "I have done all this!" It's almost as if Jesus then turns, gives him a deeper look in the eyes, and sees this young man means what he says. He sees something else, something that changes his mood entirely. Jesus looked at him and loved him. This next move is the most difficult to do well. Jesus reaches for a corner of the rug the man is standing on (or, kneeling, if you're a literalist).

"One thing you lack," he said. "Go, sell everything you have and give to the poor, and you will have treasure in heaven. Then come, follow me." At this the man's face fell. He went away sad, because he had great wealth. (vv. 21–22)

"Oh—one more thing…" The young man has an idol he is clutching in his heart. It must have been his secret love; we know from his reaction. Jesus knew by looking into his heart. In typical religious spirit posturing, the church in ages past seized this passage and made poverty a requisite for following Christ. But that misses the point entirely. Jesus had wealthy men and women among his disciples, such as Joseph of Arimathea and the women who supported the ministry. God warned the Jews many times against idolatry, that if any one set up an idol in their heart, God would set himself against them. But oh, how hard it is to topple a cherished idol.

Can you imagine how devastating this was? The young leader actually thought he had lived a thoroughly righteous life. In one comment, said almost like an afterthought, Jesus exposes him as no better than the brute heathen bowing before a wooden carving in a smoky tent, muttering prayers. Here is Jesus at his very best—he yanks this man off balance, sets his entire world reeling, and in the same moment extends his hand to catch him: "Let this go. Then come, join me. I want you to join me." What an invitation.

But the thought of giving his precious treasure away—his life-source, his security and status—it is too much for the earnest young man. He walks away, head cast down in sorrow. Exposed, but also captive to his false god. Again, wealth is not the point. The idol is the point. It might be anything—the attention of men, as with the woman at the well. Or self-righteousness, as with the religious. It might be position, power, family, even church. We craft idols faster than you can surf the Internet.

But—isn't this a story of Jesus' cunning? Does it end with the man walking away? Watch closely:

Jesus looked around and said to his disciples, "How hard it is for the rich to enter the kingdom of God!" The disciples were amazed at his words. But Jesus said again, "Children, how hard it is to enter the kingdom of God! It is easier for a camel to go through the eye of a needle than for a rich man to enter the kingdom of God." The disciples were even more amazed, and said to each other, "Who then can be saved?" Jesus looked at them and said, "With man this is impossible, but not with God; all things are possible with God." (vv. 23–27)

Picture him watching the young ruler, now at a distance, as he says these last few words. Jesus knows the sincerity of this man—there was something about him that made Jesus love him. He knows he has pulled the one thread that will unravel the whole fabric of his life. I think Jesus knows it worked. Yes, they all see the man fading from view, and the disciples are pessimistic. Jesus nods. "With man this is impossible." But he sees what they do not, sees the internal revolution already taking place, "but not with God; all things are possible with God." With a smile and a wink it's as if he says, "He'll be back." Then he turns and walks out of town.

Wow, is Jesus good.

You will appreciate the mastery of Jesus only to the degree that you understand the minefield he walks. He is advancing against the prince of darkness in a bid for the human heart. The whole situation is booby-trapped. Satan already has the upper hand—he took our hearts captive when we fell, back in Eden. Some he has snared through abuse, some through seduction, others by means of religion. Oh, how hard it is to rescue the human heart, to dislodge people from their chosen means of survival without toppling them into resignation, despair, or defensiveness.

Jesus won't take the shortcut of a power play. He doesn't force any-one to follow him. He seems rather reluctant to do his miracles. He never overwhelms anyone's will with a fantastic display of his majesty. He woos, he confronts, he delivers, he heals, he shoots straight, and then he uses intrigue. He lives out before them the most compelling view of God, shows them an incredibly attractive holiness while shat-tering the religious glaze. But still, he lets them walk away if they choose.

Now, Satan has an ace up his sleeve—even if his captives want out of the POW camp, he has a legal claim to them. A claim that can be broken only by blood. These prisoners can be ransomed, but only at a terrible price.

It appears the evil one doesn't understand Jesus' next move. He sees an opportunity to finish what he started back in the massacre of the innocents. The authorities grab Jesus at night, bring him in under false charges, bribe witnesses, then get a weary, cynical Roman puppet to execute him because the mob is about to riot. Jesus seems to have run out of options, lost his ability to maneuver. Yet this plays right into his plan—his secret plot to overthrow the rule of the evil one on earth. Apparently, Satan did *not* know that by sacrificing Jesus he would pull the one pin that would crumble his entire kingdom, fall into the very scheme God the Father had carefully, ever so carefully arranged for the undoing of evil: "We speak of God's secret wisdom, a wisdom that has been hidden and that God destined for our glory before time began. None of the rulers of this age understood it, for if they had, they would not have crucified the Lord of glory" (1 Cor. 2:7–8).

You bet they wouldn't. It ruined everything—from a certain point of view.

Now, perhaps this is nothing new to you; perhaps you've seen a bit of this before. But bring it into the present—do we love Jesus for his cunning? I don't recall a worship song with the word *cunning* in it. "Thou Art Cunning," or "Cunning, Cunning, Cunning." Do we interpret his actions in our lives as perhaps part of some cunning plan? That delayed answer to prayer—is there something brilliant about the timing? Would it help us to rest if we thought so? When he answers our prayers with "No," do we see him sparing us some unseen danger? And when it comes to our own "imitation of Christ," do we approach our days wondering, *How would Jesus have me be snakelike today?* Doesn't it sound a little unchristian?

We don't appreciate Jesus' cunning because we insist on clinging to our naive view of the world. We just want life to be easy; we just want life to be good. We don't want to deal with evil, so we pretend we don't have to. We don't want to navigate sin either. We prefer our coffeehouse chitchat, our Twitter-level engagement. We play at church.

It's as though we think our mission and our context is something other than what it was for Jesus. Even though he said, "As the Father has sent me, I am sending you" (John 20:21).

Jesus told his disciples: "There was a rich man whose manager was accused of wasting his possessions. So he called him in and asked him, 'What is this I hear about you? Give an account of your management, because you cannot be manager any longer.' The manager said to himself, 'What shall I do now? My master is taking away my job. I'm not strong enough to dig, and I'm ashamed to beg—I know what I'll do so that, when I lose my job here, people will welcome me into their houses.'

"So he called in each one of his master's debtors. He asked the first, 'How much do you owe my master?' 'Eight hundred gallons of olive oil,' he replied. The manager told him, 'Take your bill, sit down quickly, and make it four hundred.' Then he asked the second, 'And how much do you owe?' 'A thousand bushels of wheat,' he replied. He told him, 'Take your bill and make it eight hundred.' The master commended the dishonest manager because he had acted shrewdly. For the people of this world are more shrewd in dealing with their own kind than are the people of the light. I tell you, use worldly wealth to gain friends for yourselves, so that when it is gone, you will be welcomed into eternal dwellings." (LUKE 16:1–9)

Jesus is more impressed with the cunning of "the people of this world" than he is the naïveté so common to "the people of the light." And then—back to the doves and snakes analogy—he urges us to be cunning: "I want you to be smart in the same way...not complacently just get by on good behavior" (v. 9, The Message). There's a certain charm to a Forrest Gump naïveté, the kind your grandmother had as she wore her white gloves to church—but is that the kind of person you could trust with your life?

God's response to the Tower of Babel uprising was cunning—confusing the languages of the earth. It was certainly better than taking away the faculty of speech. Men could make some headway, but they would have a heck of a time uniting the world again in a rebellion against God.

Setting eternity in our hearts was cunning, so that every last one of us would be haunted all our days with unmet longings that would cause us to seek the only Fountain that can quench our thirst.

Sex was cunning. Given the selfishness and self-centeredness of mankind, how else to get people to commit to the daily-sacrifice-for-a-lifetime called parenting?

I think the movement of the Spirit in the church is cunning—first here, then there, keeping men from systemizing it, keeping the enemy from squelching it. It's like a game of rugby.

Jesus is holy and cunning—it's part of what makes me love him.

CHAPTER TEN

HUMILITY

We've been running to and fro in the Gospels, picking up one treasure, then dashing off to find another, like children on Christmas
morning. Now I want to look at a moment from Jesus' life that is
recorded in the Old Testament, in the book of Daniel. This honest
prophet—who spent his adult years an exile serving the Babylonian
courts—was given a number of startling glimpses into the future.
Here, in my opinion, is the most dazzling of them all:

> In my vision at night I looked, and there before me was one like
> a son of man, coming with the clouds of heaven. He approached
> the Ancient of Days and was led into his presence. He was given
> authority, glory and sovereign power; all peoples, nations and
> men of every language worshiped him. His dominion is an

everlasting dominion that will not pass away, and his kingdom is one that will never be destroyed. (DANIEL 7:13–14)

The coronation of Jesus.

Perhaps the most joyful, certainly the most triumphant moment in history, second only to the resurrection. For now the glorious kingdom will come, the eternal summer romp of men and angels. His crowning ensures the triumph of a kingdom of laughter and beauty and life, forever. But it was a long and circuitous road to that throne. No king has ever taken such a humble path. His first step is a staggering descent—the Son of God becomes a son of man:

Let the same mind be in you that was in Christ Jesus, who, though he was in the form of God, did not regard equality with God as something to be exploited, but emptied himself, taking the form of a slave, being born in human likeness. And being found in human form, he humbled himself and became obedient. (PHILIPPIANS 2:5–8 NRSV)

"Humbled himself?"

"Humility" hardly begins to describe the incarnation.

That's like saying it would be a humble thing for you to become a goldfish, to live in the bowl, in a fishy world, trying to help those other fishies become something more like Phoenixes. It boggles the mind. The eternal Son of God, "Light of Light, Very God of Very God...one substance with the Father," spent nine months developing in Mary's uterus. Jesus passed through her birth canal. He had to learn to walk. The Word of God had to learn to talk. He who calls the stars by name had to learn the names of everything, just as you did. "This is a cup. Can you say cup? Cuuup."

Or did you think baby Jesus came into the world with the vocabulary of Dictionary.com?

For ages upon ages, his generous hand fed every creature on earth; now it is he that has to be fed, spoon-fed, drooling most of it down his chin like any other toddler. The Son of God doesn't even know how to tie his shoes. Someone had to teach him how to tie those sandals John the Baptist said none of us were worthy to untie. "The rabbit goes around the tree and down through the hole...like that. Now you try it." Picture seven-year-old Jesus in the shop out back, learning from Joseph how to use a hammer and a saw. He who hung galaxies in such perfect poise, like a hundred billion mobiles, has to be shown how to nail two boards together.

I take my shoes off. The humility of this is beyond words.

Remember—Jesus wasn't faking it when he took on his humanity. Think of the implications. He who never tires, never slumbers, accepted the need for sleep. Every night. How deep was the exhaustion that kept him dozing right through the gale, waves crashing over the boat? Jesus ate, every day, breakfast, lunch, and dinner; he needed to. He had to trim his toenails. He who clothes the lilies of the field with greater glory than Solomon's splendor had to do his laundry, squatting riverside, rinsing the dust from his worn garments like any other peasant.

What about the humility of simply getting from here to there by means of *walking*?

We read that Jesus "left Judea and went back once more to Galilee" (John 4:3) and don't pause to wonder—how far was that? More than *70 miles*. A two- to three-day journey on foot, pushing sunup to sundown. If you bypass Samaria—which most Jews did—it was a four-to five-day trip of 120 miles. When was the last time you walked three or four days straight? We pass right over phrases such as "Jesus went up to Jerusalem" (John 2:13), as though it happened quick as we read it, like he ran across the street for a quart of milk. Bethany to Cana is roughly sixty miles; back down to Jerusalem is another forty-five plus. Jesus is making these trips all the time. He who once rode "on the wings of the wind" (Ps. 104:3) is now getting around only as fast as his two sore feet will carry him. Hours and hours, for days and months upon end, just . . . walking.

God—who is in all places at all times—has to get from one place to another like a guy who can't even come up with bus fare. The beauty of this is enough to make me weep.

When time comes for Jesus to start the official campaign, here is how he enters public life:

> In those days John the Baptist came, preaching in the Desert of Judea and saying, "Repent, for the kingdom of heaven is near." This is he who was spoken of through the prophet Isaiah: "A voice of one calling in the desert, 'Prepare the way for the Lord, make straight paths for him.'" John's clothes were made of camel's hair, and he had a leather belt around his waist. His food was locusts and wild honey. People went out to him from Jerusalem and all Judea and the whole region of the Jordan. Confessing their sins, they were baptized by him in the Jordan River. . . . Then Jesus came from Galilee to the Jordan to be baptized by John. But John tried to deter him, saying, "I need to be baptized by you, and do you come to me?" Jesus replied, "Let it be so now; it is proper for us to do this to fulfill all righteousness." Then John consented. (MATTHEW 3:1–6, 13–16)

Throngs are flooding to the Jordan to be baptized by John; the "whole region" is making their way to the river. Jesus files down bankside with the rest of the crowd and takes a place in line. Nobody gives him a second glance. He's just another sun-baked Jew in robe and sandals, taking his turn like a guy at a deli waiting for his number to be called. John looks up from his several-hundredth baptizee, and sees Jesus standing there. He is flabbergasted. He protests: "Never in a million years could I do this." Jesus says, "It's fine. This is a good thing. It's all right." Then he steps into the river and John dunks him like the rest.

It is an absolutely unimpressive story when compared with the men who think they've come to change the world. How do they usually get things rolling? Picture the scene in the movie *Gladiator*—typical to the inauguration of Roman emperors—where Commodus rides into Rome on a chariot like a conquering hero. Cheering mobs line the roads—paid to attend to make a good impression. Amid all the hollow pomp, the pompous fool gives a demur wave, feigning humble acceptance of the throne. It is appalling in its arrogance.

When Saddam Hussein was ousted from his dictatorship, a good deal of coverage was given to public places in Iraq. What I found particularly disgraceful were the massive idols he had erected in his honor. Murals and statues of Hussein the Magnificent were plastered all over the country—a handsome and dashing military hero, bold, a man for the people, forty years younger than he actually was. A demigod. Many dictators have done the same. Hitler did it; Chairman Mao too. It's just creepy—the self-obsession, self-exaltation, the desire to be worshipped. Yet the only king who ever had a right to be worshipped shows up riverside at somebody's else's revival and waits his turn.

Afterward there is no press conference, no sermon. Jesus just disappears for forty days, and the only one who seems to notice is the wild Baptist in the camel skin. A day or two after his return, Jesus is just strolling by and John—gripped with excitement—seizes his own pupils by the shoulders and says, "Look! Look! There he is!"

> The next day John again was standing with two of his disciples, and as he watched Jesus walk by, he exclaimed, "Look, here is the Lamb of God!" The two disciples heard him say this, and they followed Jesus. When Jesus turned and saw them follow-ing, he said to them, "What are you looking for?" They said to him, "Rabbi" (which translated means Teacher), "where are you staying?" He said to them, "Come and see." They came and saw where he was staying, and they remained with him that day. It was about four o'clock in the afternoon. (JOHN 1:35–39 NRSV)

"Rabbi, where are you staying?" Oh, come *on*—is that what they really want to ask?! Their master just bet it all on this man. Don't you think they're dying to ask, "*Are* you the Son of God? Our Messiah? Are you really the Lamb who takes away the sin of the world?!" This is a once-in-a-lifetime opportunity. Jesus sees that he is being fol-lowed, and in his typical fashion he simply says, "Can I help you?," smiling, head cocked, eyebrows raised. They must have been flum-moxed, like you would be, because they ask the lamest question: "Where are you staying?" That's the question kindergartners ask one another on the first day of school: "Where do *you* live?" Jesus disarms their fumbling awe by saying, "Come and see." Not "Oh, here and there," not "Over on the other side of town." C'mon, I'll show ya.

Humble and inviting.

Andrew races off to find Peter, Philip runs to get Nathanael, and the little band begins to coalesce. They wander up to Galilee, where

Jesus taps James and John. None of them know it yet, but they will become the most famous band of brothers in the world. Thus Jesus starts his ministry. We've all heard the story and missed the miracle—God begins his greatest work by including us. Even though we bungled it so badly the first time, back in Eden. Once again he shares in the excitement. Come with me, you have a part in this—the re-creation of the world.

Can you name one world leader who has done anything even close to this? What were the names of Buddha's disciples? Gandhi's? George Washington's? Apart from a few history buffs, none of us can even name one. But everyone who hears about Jesus hears about "the Twelve," and can probably name Peter, Matthew, James and John, certainly Judas. Jesus and "his disciples" go hand in hand. Right here from the start, he acts like it's not all about him. He shares the stage, shares the spotlight. He shares his glory: "I have given them the glory that you gave me" (John 17:22). He even shares his suffering. The crown of thorns, the cross—is this not the noblest part of his whole life, the very thing we most worship him for? Even in this he offers to us, "the fellowship of sharing in his sufferings" (Phil. 3:10). It is an honor I cannot begin to fathom.

The humility of this is so...humbling. It just takes my breath away.

Once chosen, Jesus then needs to disciple these fishermen, tax collectors, and political revolutionaries who dropped their careers to follow him. I'm not sure we've understood the ramifications of his decision. We just think, *Oh, yeah, the disciples,* and forget what was actually required for them to *become* apostles. This is going to take a lot of work. There's no fairy godmother waving her wand here; these pumpkins don't just turn into coaches. To show you just what sort of patience and long-suffering it took to train these knuckleheads, let's drop in on two private conversations Jesus has with his apprentices. (I love it that these were recorded for posterity.)

This first one takes place maybe a day after the boys helped Jesus feed a crowd of four thousand–plus using seven loaves and "a few small fish." (It cracks me up that "small" is underscored, as if it would have been easier with a few larger fish.) They personally handed out the bread that kept multiplying in their hands; they gathered up the seven basketfuls afterward. As they head out of town Jesus has another run-in with the religious leaders, those sanctified Machiavellis, and he's getting pretty sick of it. They demand from him a sign; Jesus says they're not going to get one. He then turns and warns the boys about the infectious corruption of the religious haze.

> When they went across the lake, the disciples forgot to take bread. "Be careful," Jesus said to them. "Be on your guard against the yeast of the Pharisees and Sadducees." They discussed this among themselves and said, "It is because we didn't bring any bread." (MATTHEW 16:5–7)

How many of these little whispered asides take place between the disciples over the years? *"Simon, what do you think he meant by that?"* This one is priceless. Somebody whispers, *"He's mad at us because we forgot to bring bread."* Okay—even *if* Jesus was talking about bread, how could they possibly worry about bread anymore? They've seen Jesus handle that problem with staggering ease. Yesterday. But Jesus didn't mention bread. How did they make the jump from a warning about the fungus of the Pharisees to what are we going to do for dinner? It's quite a leap of logic—a jump not even Evel Knievel could make.

Oh, Jesus. How many times does a man have to explain himself? He clearly sounds frustrated. I love the next line: "Aware of their discussion, Jesus asked, 'You of little faith, why are you talking among yourselves about having no bread?' " (v. 8). Aware of their discussion— did they not notice he was in the same boat when they started this little whispered debate?—Jesus goes on:

> "Do you still not understand? Don't you remember the five loaves for the five thousand, and how many basketfuls you gathered? Or the seven loaves for the four thousand, and how many basketfuls you gathered? How is it you don't understand that I was not talking to you about bread? But be on your guard against the yeast of the Pharisees and Sadducees." Then they understood that he was not telling them to guard against the yeast used in bread, but against the teaching of the Pharisees and Sadducees. (vv. 9–12)

Ohhh. Now we get it. You were talking about their *teaching*. Honestly, sometimes these guys seem thick as an engine block.

This second anecdote takes place as Jesus is now making his way toward Jerusalem for the final showdown. He sends an advance team before him to secure a night's lodging in a Samaritan town, but the door is slammed in their faces. Furious, they return to Jesus with the report, chomping for revenge:

> On their way they entered a village of the Samaritans to make ready for him; but they did not receive him, because his face was set toward Jerusalem. When his disciples James and John saw it, they said, "Lord, do you want us to command fire to come down from heaven and consume them?" But he turned and rebuked them. Then they went on to another village. (LUKE 9:52–56 NRSV)

Well—they certainly get credit for passion. We'll give them an A for zeal. But as for comprehension…they get an F. For heaven's sake—these guys had front-row seats for the Sermon on the Mount, got private lessons on it afterward. For nearly three years now they have had Jesus as their personal tutor. No, fellas, we're not going to be torching villages. This isn't Sherman's march to the sea. Let's try this again—love your enemies. Pray for those who persecute you. Talk about exasperating. How does Jesus put up with these numskulls? It's like training the hobbits to run a country.

It proves his humility is genuine, though.

I mean, anybody can fake this for a while. To be a crowd-drawing teacher can be a rather heady experience, all eyes looking to you for the next bit of wisdom to drop from your lips. It's easy to be gracious when you're adored. But when your class keeps missing the point, challenging you, running down rabbit trails, changing the subject, misunderstanding, breaking out into a brawl—that's when your character is exposed. I never really saw the endurance of this. I think the shining brilliance of *what* Jesus is teaching has obscured the *process* involved here, all that this required of him. We've become so used to Jesus being gracious, kind, and patient, we miss the humility of it.

Now, this next turn might come as a surprise—how about the humility of the Mount of Transfiguration? Yes, humility.

For one radiant moment in Jesus' life the curtain is parted, and he is allowed a minute of undimmed presence, talking with Moses and Elijah as he must have done many times prior to his incarnation. This takes place only once in his earthly life, so far as we know. And it happens about as far from the public eye as possible—way off north of the Sea of Galilee, possibly on Mount Hermon, nearly two hundred miles from the epicenter of Jewish life in Jerusalem. There were only three witnesses, whom—in classic Jesus modesty—he immediately forbids telling anyone about it. Then it's back down the hill into the what-have-you-done-for-me-lately crowds, the late nights, sleeping in somebody else's house or barn, often in the woods, dodging the police, trying to prepare his boys to carry on after him.

Overarching all of this, running through it like a leitmotif, what Jesus primarily models for us is how to draw our life from the Father. The passage I quoted earlier from Philippians—one of the earliest hymns of the faith—says that Jesus more than humbled himself when he came to earth. He *emptied* himself:

Who, being in very nature God, did not consider equality with God something to be grasped, but made himself nothing, taking the very nature of a servant, being made in human likeness. (PHILIPPIANS 2:6–7)

Who, though he was in the form of God, did not regard equality with God as something to be exploited, but emptied himself, taking the form of a slave, being born in human likeness. (NRSV)

Though he was God, he did not think of equality with God as something to cling to. Instead, he gave up his divine privileges; he took the humble position of a slave and was born as a human being. (NLT)

The *kenosis* of Christ, a mystery we cannot fully explain nor explain away—the choice Jesus made to "empty" himself of his divine powers and prerogatives in order to take on the limitations of humanity. Now, I realize there is debate on exactly how much Jesus emptied himself, but if you believe that he wasn't "faking" his humanity (which orthodox Christians have held for two thousand years) then you must rid yourselves of the "Einstein doing first-grade math" image. If Jesus was pretending to be a man, then his life is so far beyond ours it can't really be a model for us to follow. To err is human, to forgive is divine and all that. *But*, if Jesus chose a genuine humanity, and drew his power from the Father as we must do, then we *can* live as he did. Behold:

> We do not have a high priest who is unable to sympathize with our weaknesses, but we have one who has been tempted in every way, just as we are. (HEBREWS 4:15)

> Although he was a son, he learned obedience from what he suffered. (HEBREWS 5:8)

> I tell you the truth, the Son can do nothing by himself; he can do only what he sees his Father doing. (JOHN 5:19)

> I did not speak of my own accord, but the Father who sent me commanded me what to say and how to say it. (JOHN 12:49)

Paul speaks of different glories—the glory of the sun, as compared to the glory of the moon. There are different humilities as well. You have the humility of setting aside an office—the king takes off his crown to become a pauper in the street. But there is the greater humility of setting aside the *power*—the Son of God lays down his glory to become a human being. It is the humility of utter dependence. Jesus wept, he prayed, he *learned obedience*—so that we might learn to do the same. We will come back to the implication for our lives in a moment. For now, what we are witnessing when Jesus "disciples" his followers is something like the emperor stepping down in the arena to face the lions with us, show us how it's done, using only the tools available to us. Staggering. And so hopeful.

Then comes the upper room, the dishtowel and basin, and the dirty feet of twelve confused men. You want us to do *what*?! Peter thinks he's got it figured out and asks Jesus to give him a bath. Proving that we, too, are just like the disciples, we've grabbed on to this metaphor and made it a sacrament—all the while missing the point. You can submit to the tradition and wash a few pairs of feet at church, but turn around and live a completely self-centered life, untouched by the ritual save for the fact that it grossed you out and you're planning to skip it next time.

His silence before Pilate is stunning. The cynical little martinet dares to ask Jesus, "What is truth?" (John 18:38). Jesus doesn't even bother answering. He just stares at Pilate, letting him make the next move. You know how the story goes—though Jesus says he could call down more than sixty thousand angels to prevent it, he lets them kill him, and pardons them beforehand for doing it. Because of his extraordinary humility, no one seems to fully grasp just who this is. But nature knows, and cannot bear it—the earth convulses; the sun hides his face. It is only after the resurrection that the full reality begins to dawn on mankind. If it has even dawned on us yet.

And then there comes the touching humility of keeping the scars of those wounds—forever. You'll see them, soon, get to touch them for yourself, just like Thomas. Jesus wears them proudly now.

And being found in appearance as a man, he humbled himself and became obedient to death—even death on a cross! Therefore God exalted him to the highest place and gave him the name that is above every name, that at the name of Jesus every knee should bow, in heaven and on earth and under the earth, and every tongue confess that Jesus Christ is Lord, to the glory of God the Father. (PHILIPPIANS 2:8–11)

I think three years of this kind of humble generosity and patience is pretty dang impressive. But Jesus has kept right on at it—for two thousand years. Teaching us, including us in the mission, sharing in the glory, being playful, being honest, helping us along. No wonder when he steps into the heavens to accept the throne the cry goes up, "Worthy! Worthy! Worthy! Make him king!"

This man is so worthy.

CHAPTER ELEVEN

TRUENESS

Every era has its problems when it comes to knowing Jesus. One of ours is this: Having lost all confidence in the noble, the heroic, even the consistently good, we have come to celebrate the neurotic. Really. The heroes of our novels and movies are antiheroes, broken characters riddled with addiction and self-doubt. In fact, doubt—masquerading as humility—has become a condition for acceptance in our times. People of strong conviction and bold claims are suspect. We fear them. They might be a terrorist, or a Christian.

Part of this is entirely understandable, the inevitable backlash from a glut of investigative journalism in a target-rich environment. When you live in a world rocked by scandal and exposé multiple times a day, you just grow cynical. Who is it this time—some politician, a multi-national corporation, the church? Take a number. We've reached the point where we *presume* corruption or, at least, that every story is tainted. Guilty until proven innocent. It is the triumph of jaundice. Skepticism has become a virtue.

This has quietly shaped a popular version of Jesus as a man not so much heroic as humanitarian, not a warrior operating behind enemy lines but just a humble man trying to do good in a hurting world. A man stuck in his personal Gethsemane. If he is doubting and uncertain, we feel better about ourselves. Now yes, yes—Jesus had his dark night of the soul. There was that harrowing moment on the cross where he cried out to a Father who had seemed to abandon him. But friends—this encompassed less than twenty-four hours of his entire life. He didn't live there, nor did he stay there. It was an abyss through which he passed. Through which he was *able* to pass, because of something much deeper within him.

When Jesus returns mounted on a white horse, army by his side, to end this horrific age and usher in the next, he is called by a name we haven't heard in the Gospels. That name is Faithful and True: "I saw heaven standing open and there before me was a white horse, whose rider is called Faithful and True" (Rev. 19:11). By that point in the story, it is what he deserves to be called, and it is what the world needs to be assured of, too. Faithful and true. Qualities so rare in this carnival of masquerades they will take some unpacking to appreciate.

Let us begin with a contrast—two experiences, one from private life, the other quite public.

A few years ago our family visited Europe. We were hosted by a wealthy couple known for their hospitality. As soon as we walked in the door I knew they would live up to their reputation—everyone in their home was so *warm*. The kiss on both cheeks, the place of honor at the table, the toast in our name. I found myself wondering, *Why aren't we more like this—so friendly and inviting to outsiders?* Their benevolence was almost intoxicating. As we drove away, one of my sons said, "That was creepy."

It was a jarring thing to say. It felt like an unrighteous thing to say. But it was also like the ring of the bell that breaks the spell in a fairy tale.

"Go on," I said.

"Well, yeah, they were all superfriendly. But they didn't want to know me. No one asked one meaningful question. It was a false intimacy," he explained.

And indeed it was, though the truth was so very hard to recognize when you were in the midst of it. Especially when their reputation—several friends had dined at their home—was so untarnished. Then we realized that this was precisely the point—it was the *image* of warmth and intimacy that was important. Such experiences can be crazy-making, because it *feels* so gracious and it *feels* so wrong to question it. Aha—now we are closing in. It feels wrong to question it. That begins to expose the underlying motive.

As Jesus well knows, a kiss is not always what it seems to be.

Not long afterward, I attended a conference with about ten thousand other people. The roster of speakers included a number of "all-star" Christian leaders. First up was a man that would be described as "on the cutting edge" of what is happening in the church today. Young, gifted, and very hip. He spent the majority of his allotted time telling two unrelated stories. The first was a funny and dramatic account of how he helped a homeless woman get some food. The story felt a little out of context because his sermon wasn't about homelessness. But it *was* a very cool story. His second tale was even more so. It centered around a wild bit of foreign travel that wound him up in the midst of the international Formula One racing circuit. Really impressive—though it had no tie whatsoever to the first story, nor to his point.

But the overall effect—what you might call the "gravitational pull" of the illustrations—was to think that Christianity can be very cool. Not to mention (time for that demur wave) that this guy was very, very cool as well.

Now, I am not judging this man. I am attempting to name something deep in human nature. Something I know too well in myself. For I know the inside of this world—not merely the insides of the *culture* of Christian conferences (sometimes a religious Las Vegas), but also the inside of the *hearts* of Christian speakers (an even more contradictory world than Vegas). For I am one.

Consider the natural human longing to be loved and admired, how deep it runs in you. It is practically an aching abyss. Remember how rare it is for love and admiration to come to any soul in this jealous world. Now, add to this poverty the insight that very gifted people actually have a *greater* need for affirmation than most (it's true). You begin to feel how intoxicating it is to have thousands of people holding their breath for the next word you have to speak.

Now, mix into this high-altitude experience two other seductions. Given the horrible things that *do* go on in the name of Jesus Christ, it is deeply seducing among Christian leaders to come across way too humble and hip and genuine for that. While at the same time it is rather nice to have your audience think you are so very cool for having introduced them to such a cool Jesus. Heroin and pornography are child's play compared to this stuff.

Jesus cuts to the heart in one sentence:

He who speaks on his own does so to gain honor for himself, but he who works for the honor of the one who sent him is a man of truth; there is nothing false about him. (JOHN 7:18)

Ouch.

I wonder how much of what takes place in Christendom could actually pass this test as true. Nothing false about it? Some days you would be hard-pressed to find something true about it. There's more holes here than in Swiss cheese.

The issue is one of *motives*.

Why did Nicodemus visit Jesus *at night*? Fear of what his peers would do if they found out. He wasn't alone in this; John says that "many even among the leaders believed in him. But because of the Pharisees they would not confess their faith for fear they would be put out of the synagogue" (12:42). They chose job security over Jesus. This fear is a mighty powerful force. Even after their son is healed of blindness—and how grateful would a mother and father be?!—even then the fellow's parents tremble before the elite:

> The Jews still did not believe that he had been blind and had received his sight until they sent for the man's parents. "Is this your son?" they asked. "Is this the one you say was born blind? How is it that now he can see?"
>
> "We know he is our son," the parents answered, "and we know he was born blind. But how he can see now, or who opened his eyes, we don't know. Ask him. He is of age; he will speak for himself." His parents said this because they were afraid of the Jews, for already the Jews had decided that anyone who acknowledged that Jesus was the Christ would be put out of the synagogue. (JOHN 9:18–22)

The fear of man. Peer pressure. What will others think? This can get deadly. Look at how this forces Herod to execute John:

On Herod's birthday the daughter of Herodias danced for them and pleased Herod so much that he promised with an oath to give her whatever she asked. Prompted by her mother, she said, "Give me here on a platter the head of John the Baptist." The king was distressed, *but because of his oaths and his dinner guests*, he ordered that her request be granted and had John beheaded in the prison. (MATTHEW 14:6–10, italics added)

Because of his dinner guests?! He had an innocent man guillotined because of his *dinner guests*?!!

I'm convinced that until we have a healthy appreciation of how deep this actually runs in us, we are kidding ourselves about our motives.

I made a quick list of things "I would never be caught dead doing." It includes: getting a pedicure; having my personal journals read from the podium at the National Religious Broadcasters Convention; yodeling on *Oprah* in a tutu. The fear is way beyond reason; it is gut-level, primal. You have your list, and I have mine. This fear runs deep in the human race. It is ancient, Genesis 3:10 stuff—"I was afraid because I was naked; so I hid." The fear of exposure. It is far more powerful than we like to admit—the origin of every fig leaf and fashion trend. It's what gives power to culture. We long to be praised. We dread exposure.

Everyone from high school students to CEOs is jumping on the "Green" bandwagon right now. Green is in; Green is enlightened; Green is the cause du jour. Every corporation from coffee to cars now sells itself as Green. Huh. They didn't do this five years ago—how come they're suddenly touting their Green credentials now? Do you honestly think this is all in the humble interest of a better world? Then why don't they just do it, and not tell anyone about it? (Isn't that what Jesus said in the Sermon on the Mount?!)

So—motives are essential, and motives are often, shall we say, questionable.

Surely you remember high school. Did you really wear whatever clothes you wanted, say whatever you believed when you went to school? Heavens no. You'd have been eaten alive. It's a shark tank, a pack of jackals—one show of weakness and you will be devoured by your own kind. We dressed and spoke and laughed and walked and held the opinions we did so as to fit "in." Our group of choice may have been the jocks, the cool kids, the academic crowd, the rebels. Regardless of the details, we all lived a very calculated life.

We still do.

"What people think of me" is a *very* powerful motivator. It is still shaping us more than we'd like to admit. It shapes our theology, our politics, our values. I spent time today with a young man in the music industry; why did I use the term "dude" more than I usually do? Before that, I was speaking with a woman in ministry; I never used the term "dude," but I did talk about "the Lord" a good bit. I feel like a chameleon. I "adapt" myself to the social foliage around me.

Do any of us go through one entire day being utterly true no matter how many different environments we move through? Do you even know the true you? *Is* there a true you? Whether it is born of fear or longing or uncertainty or cunning or wickedness, it so natural for us to shape ourselves according to the moment we scarcely notice how much we do it. Now, toss in the promise of reward—wealth, power, success, the adoration of others—and boy, oh boy, is it hard to be true.

Friends—surely you are aware that your *personality* has a *motive* behind it?

Only when you have taken an honest look inside yourself, and seen what really fuels the things you do, will you appreciate how utterly remarkable it is to be true. And how utterly desirable. We are given the story of Jesus' wilderness trial to help us understand that Jesus has been tried—and proven true. Remember now, Jesus wasn't cheating; it was a genuine test of his character, so profoundly terrible, to be seduced by the evil one himself, that Jesus needed angels to minister to him afterward.

We typically think of integrity as the ability to resist temptation by resolve. And that's a good thing; self-discipline is a good thing. But there is another level of integrity, the kind where you don't even *want* the seduction that is being presented to you. Goodness runs so deep, so pervasive through your character and your being that you don't even want it. We respect the man who is able to reject sexual temptation. But how much more the man whose soul is such that he does not want any woman but the woman he loves and is married to.

Let's come back to what makes us false—the lion's share of it is motivated by a fear of man. Someone just texted me; I agreed to meet them tomorrow for lunch. Now, the truth is, I'd really rather not. I honestly don't have the time. So why did I say yes? Fear of disappointing; fear of being *thought of* as disappointing; fear that next time, when it is me asking for a favor, this person will say no. I wince to think of how much I do out of the fear of man.

> While Jesus was still talking to the crowd, his mother and brothers stood outside, wanting to speak to him. Someone told him, "Your mother and brothers are standing outside, wanting to speak to you." He replied to him, "Who is my mother, and who are my brothers?" Pointing to his disciples, he said, "Here are my mother and my brothers. For whoever does the will of my Father in heaven is my brother and sister and mother." (MATTHEW 12:46–50)

Oh my. The Jewish culture may be *the* most family-centric culture in the world. "Honor your father and mother" has been drilled into Jewish sons and daughters from birth. Back at the wedding reception, all Mary had to do was turn and say, "They're out of wine," and Jesus made the exception, for her. A Jewish mother and a good Jewish boy. Here we have Jesus inside a crowded house teaching; word gets passed through the crowd: "Your mother and your brothers are outside," and everyone understands what he will do next—he'll stop what he's doing and go to them.

He doesn't. He leaves them standing in the street.

Now remember—you are watching love. Here is another portrait of love in action. Whatever else we see, we see Jesus is not beholden even to family. Maybe some of you are free in this regard (are you sure it's not merely defiance?) but it is absolutely extraordinary for the rest of us. "You're going to be here for Christmas this year, of course— you know how much it means to your mother." "It's been two weeks since you called—is everything all right?" "Your brother needs a place to stay for a few months—we know you'll do the right thing." How much of what we do is motivated by fear of man? Think of it— to be entirely free of false guilt, free from pressure, from false allegiances. It would be absolutely extraordinary.

This is what gives Jesus the ability to say such startlingly honest things to people.

It is what enables him to be so scandalous.

This is the secret of his ability to navigate praise and contempt.

Neither success nor opposition have power over him. One day the crowds love him, the next they are shouting for his crucifixion. Jesus is the same man—the same *personality*—through the whole swirling tempest. Jesus is free from the fear of man. It is something more than integrity, though it certainly encompasses that. He is true to himself, true to his Father, true to what the moment most requires, true to love. In this forest of fig leaves, where you are never sure you are getting the true person, there is nothing false about Jesus.

That alone makes me adore him.

Nobody likes being lied to. Notice your outrage when some trusted leader is exposed as a fake. Think of how strong your reaction is when a close friend lies to you. Some relationships never recover. Now—it is one thing to tell a lie; it is something else entirely to *be* a lie. The man who has two families, carries on two separate lives—he's not just lying about what he does, he's lying about what he *is*.

The most essential gift you have to give is yourself. When you aren't entirely true about that, you aren't true. But we've all grown accustomed to committing dozens of little white lies about ourselves every day.

Except this man. He is Faithful and he is True.

Having given this some thought, perhaps we are better prepared now to understand why God answered Moses the way he did when he spoke from the burning bush. In the midst of the very unnerving encounter, Moses asks him, "Who *are* you?" God simply says, "I Am." In other words, Me. Myself. An answer that is holy and full of integrity, wry and dumbfounding all at the same time. But it is the best possible answer he could have given. God is utterly himself.

I love Lewis's allegory of this in the Narnian tale *The Horse and His Boy*. Shasta, the reluctant boy hero of the story, finds himself at the end of a harrowing journey lost and alone in a forest in the middle of a foggy night. A mysterious figure has come alongside him and begun to explain to Shasta the meaning of his life. The boy does not yet know it is the Great Lion, Aslan.

"I do not call you unfortunate," said the Large Voice. "Don't you think it was bad luck to meet so many lions?" said Shasta. "There was only one lion," said the Voice. "What on earth do you mean? I've just told you there were at least two the first night, and—" "There was only one: but he was swift of foot." "How do you know?" "I was the lion." And as Shasta gaped with open mouth and said nothing, the Voice continued. "I was the lion who forced you to join with Aravis. I was the cat who comforted you among the houses of the dead. I was the lion who drove the jackals from you while you slept. I was the lion who gave the Horses the new strength of fear for the last mile so that you should reach King Lune in time. And I was the lion you do not remember who pushed the boat in which you lay, a child near death, so that it came to shore where a man sat, wakeful at midnight, to receive you."

"Then it was you who wounded Aravis?" "It was I." "But what for?" "Child," said the Voice, "I am telling you your story, not hers. I tell no one any story but his own." "Who *are* you," asked Shasta. "Myself," said the Voice, very deep and low so that the earth shook; and again "Myself" loud and clear and gay; and then the third time "Myself," whispered so softly you could hardly hear it, and yet it seemed to come from all round you as if the leaves rustled with it...

The mist was turning from black to gray and from gray to white. This must have begun to happen some time ago, but while he had been talking to the Thing he had not been noticing anything else. Now, the whiteness around him became a shining whiteness; his eyes began to blink. Somewhere ahead he could hear birds singing. He knew the night was over at last.

He could see the mane and ears and head of his horse quite easily now. A golden light fell on them from the left. He thought it was the sun. He turned and saw, pacing beside him, taller than the horse, a Lion. The horse did not seem to be afraid of it or else could not see it. It was from the Lion that the light came. No one ever saw anything more terrible or beautiful.[1]

Who *are* you? "Myself."

Jesus is simply himself. Playful, cunning, generous, fierce—not one moment of it is contrived. He never plays to the audience, never kowtows to the opposition, never takes his cues from the circus around him. He is simply being himself.

I think this will help us with one of the confounding experiences we have reading the Gospels.

The diversity of Jesus' actions, timing, manner, words, dare we say moods; his sudden changes of direction, then his stillness—it's hard to keep up with. It certainly is colorful, but almost dizzying, like a Byzantine mosaic, alive and shifting like the northern lights. Dazzling, but nearly to the point of leaving us confused. As soon as we've grabbed on to one dimension of Jesus—his generosity, his compassion, his honesty—he seems to turn it on its head, or us on ours. I was the lion that forced you to join with Aravis, the cat who comforted you in the tombs, the lion who drove the jackals from you, and the same lion who gave your horses new strength of fear.

Perhaps the Gospel stories seem dizzying only because we've never seen anyone act like this before. Maybe what we are witnessing is actually one single quality, not many. Maybe Jesus is simply being true.

Who *are* you? "Myself." It is this that makes me love him more than anything else.

I wonder if this response doesn't shed some light on one of the most famous and inscrutable moments in Jesus' famous and often misinterpreted life—that bit about him walking on water:

> When evening came, his disciples went down to the lake, where they got into a boat and set off across the lake for Capernaum. By now it was dark, and Jesus had not yet joined them. A strong wind was blowing and the waters grew rough. When they had rowed three or three and a half miles, they saw Jesus approaching the boat, walking on the water; and they were terrified. But he said to them, "It is I; don't be afraid." Then they were willing to take him into the boat, and immediately the boat reached the shore where they were heading. The next day the crowd that had stayed on the opposite shore of the lake realized that only one boat had been there, and that Jesus had not entered it with his disciples, but that they had gone away alone. (JOHN 6:16–22)

What do we have here, really? Most of the time Jesus seems reluctant to perform miracles, and when he does do them he usually insists that no one be told. He certainly was no show-off. But this—good grief, this is so *flagrant*. What was this about? Well, stay with the facts of the story; they are always provided for a reason. There was one and only one boat. The disciples took it and headed straight across the lake for the opposite shore—more than three and a half miles, as the crow flies. Jesus lingered to dismiss the crowd, and then to pray on the mountain. This is actually the continuation of the scene after John's death, when Jesus tried to get away by himself to grieve. But the crowds intercepted him. Though brokenhearted, Jesus healed them, fed them, then sent them on their way and sent the disciples off with the only boat. Finally, he was able to be alone.

Now it is hours later, late into the night, and Jesus comes walking on the water.

It may be that he wanted to demonstrate in a rather unforgettable way his power over nature. But—the disciples had just received a major dose of that. This very day he fed the five thousand from a lunchbox. They've seen him shut down a storm on this very sea. They've seen him raise the dead. Plenty of that lesson, and more to come at the resurrection.

On the other hand, we do know this: He intended to cross. It is roughly twenty five miles to reach the Capernaum by walking the shoreline. That would take an entire day. Maybe Jesus simply took the shortcut. After all, the shortest distance between two points *is* a straight line. He didn't fly. He just...walked, and the lake happened to be there. Maybe he was simply being himself.

CHAPTER TWELVE

BEAUTIFUL

There are certain people you would want by your side if you were summoned to appear in court.

And then there are others you want to take with you to a party. You can probably think of one or two folks you'd want to be with if you had to walk through a rough part of town. Then there are the gems you'd love to have join you on vacation. If you are lucky, you know a few rare souls you would feel completely comfortable calling at 2:00 a.m. to share your suffering. The people you want to entrust with your surgery or the care of your children might not be the ones who come to mind when playing the old game "Whom would you take if you knew you were going to be stranded on a desert island?" They are very rarely the same person. Right?

We all know brilliant minds who could do with a touch of humility, humble folk who ought to stand up for themselves, driven types who need to lighten up, jokesters who should grow up, and gracious souls who really ought to get good and mad once in a while. My lawyer ought to take dance lessons and the dance instructor needs a little more—how do I say this? Backbone.

But imagine if you found it all in one person—superb before a jury, terrific taste in movies, ready at the drop of a hat for a riot of a vacation, and also able to handle your deepest, darkest secrets. Wouldn't you want this person to be your friend?!

Jesus is this man. Remember now these snapshots; imagine them; take your time and bring each one before your mind's eye:

On the beach, catching the boys fishing.
Clearing the temple.
Touching the man with leprosy—after his famous sermon.
Infuriating the Pharisees by healing on the Sabbath.
Midday at the Samaritan well.
Before Lazarus's tomb.
Losing his cousin.
Late in the reception at Cana.
Dinner with Martha.
Learning to use a hammer and nail.
All those miles by foot.
His own trial and torture.
And then—the Emmaus road.

The vast richness of this man is…enthralling.

When I first became a Christian more than thirty-two years ago, the little church group I found myself in sang a worship song that went, "Beautiful, beautiful, Jesus is beautiful." I joined in wholeheart-edly, sensing it was true, but not quite certain what it meant, really. Were they saying that Jesus is good-looking?

Now I understand.

To say that Jesus is perfect—as the "defenders of his glory" do—isn't the right choice of words. A stainless-steel ball is perfect; Cinderella's glass slipper was perfect; a haiku is perfect. Perfect makes me think of Barbie, a Grecian urn, a math equation. Words are important. Words shape our perceptions. When they define, they can also distort. There is a far better way to describe this man whose face is the most human face of all.

Jesus is beautiful.

His ability to live with all these qualities we've seen, in such a way that no one quality dominates—as is so often the case in our personalities—eclipsing the richness of the others. To live in such a way that there is always something of an element of surprise, and yet, however he acts turns out to be exactly what was needed in the moment. Oh, his brilliance shines through, but never blinding, never overbearing. He is not glistening white marble. He is the playfulness of creation, scandal and utter goodness, the generosity of the ocean and the ferocity of a thunderstorm; he is cunning as a snake and gentle as a whisper; the gladness of sunshine and the humility of a thirty-mile walk by foot on a dirt road. Reclining at a meal, laughing with friends, and then going to the cross.

That is what we mean when we say Jesus is beautiful.

But most of all, it is the way he loves. In all these stories, every encounter, we have watched love in action. Love as strong as death; a blood, sweat, and tears love, not a get-well card. You learn a great deal about the true nature of a person in the way they love, why they love, and, in what they love.

While Jesus was in Bethany in the home of a man known as Simon the Leper, a woman came to him with an alabaster jar of very expensive perfume, which she poured on his head as he was reclining at the table. When the disciples saw this, they were indignant. "Why this waste?" they asked. "This perfume could have been sold at a high price and the money given to the poor." Aware of this, Jesus said to them, "Why are you bothering this woman? She has done a beautiful thing to me. The poor you will always have with you, but you will not always have me. When she poured this perfume on my body, she did it to prepare me for burial. I tell you the truth, wherever this gospel is preached throughout the world, what she has done will also be told, in memory of her." (MATTHEW 26:6–13)

She has done a beautiful thing indeed.

But it takes a beautiful heart to recognize the beauty in a scandalous act, and to love it as he does. This is why we say Jesus is beautiful. A Beautiful Outlaw.

"This changes everything." A good friend of mine was reading the manuscript as I passed along chapters to him. At this point, he put the book down and said, "This means everything. This changes everything."

It does. It will.

But only if you find him for yourself.

All of this is merely entertaining unless it opens the door for us to experience Jesus. The best thing we can do now is pause, before we are saturated with more information about Jesus, and begin to discover him for ourselves. Experience him personally *in these ways*.

"Come and see," as Philip said to Nathanael (John 1:46). Come and see for yourself.

CHAPTER THIRTEEN

LOVING JESUS

Friends, this is not simply a nicer view of Jesus. This is not merely a more winsome Christ or a smattering of fresh insights. This is not confetti—lovely while it falls, soon to be swept away.

Jesus is our *life*.

We need Jesus like we need oxygen. Like we need water. Like the branch needs the vine. Jesus is not merely a figure for devotions. He is the missing essence of your existence. Whether we know it or not, we are desperate for Jesus.

What if you could have Jesus the way Peter and John had him? The way Mary and Lazarus did?

I said at the outset of this book that to have Jesus, really have him, is to have the greatest treasure in all worlds. To have his life, joy, love, and presence cannot be compared. To know him as he is, is to come home. A true knowledge of Jesus is our greatest need and our greatest happiness. The purpose of your being here on this planet, at this moment in time, comes down to three things:

1. To love Jesus with all that is within you. This is the first and greatest command. Everything else flows from here.
2. To share your daily life with him; to let him be himself with you. On the beach, at supper, along the road—just as the disciples did.
3. To allow his life to fill yours, to heal and express itself through yours. There is no other way you can hope to live as he did and show him to others.

Love Jesus. Let him be himself with you. Allow his life to permeate yours. The fruit of this will be...breathtaking.

Now for the best news you will ever receive. O, how I wish this book had a sound track, because the orchestra would resound here with a crash, and then go utterly silent as you read these next words: You get to.

You get to.

You are *meant* to have this Jesus, more than you have each new day, more than you have your next breath. For heaven's sake—he *is* your next day, your next breath. You are *meant* to share life with him—not just a glimpse now and then at church, not just a rare sighting. And you are *meant* to live his life. The purpose of his life, death, and resurrection was to ransom you from your sin, deliver you from the clutches of evil, restore you to God—*so that* his personality and his life could heal and fill your personality, your humanity, and your life. This is the reason he came.

Anything else is religion.

Sadly, for too many people, the Christ they know is too religious to love, too distant to experience, and too rigid to be a source of life. It explains the abject poverty of the church. But hear this—Jesus hasn't changed one bit. He is still quite himself. This is still how he acts. The Scriptures assure us that Jesus is the same yesterday, today, and forever (Hebrews 13:8). This is how he presented himself; this is who he is. God is better than we thought. Much better than we feared. Better even than we dared to believe.

MAKE A PRACTICE OF LOVING JESUS

So, the best thing you can do at this point is simply begin to love Jesus.

Just love him.

It will open up your heart and soul to experiencing him, and to receiving his life. Just begin to make a practice of loving Jesus. As I'm driving in my car, I will simply tell him, "I love you." Not once, like a sneeze, but over and over again: "I love you, I love you, I love you." It turns my whole being toward him in love. When I wake up and the sunshine is pouring through the window, I'll say, "I love you." I'll look at a photograph of some fond memory, or some beautiful place, and I'll say, "I love you." A breeze will caress my face ever so gently, and I'll turn into it and say, "I love you." Anytime something makes me laugh. When I see a chipmunk or a wave, when I enjoy a movie. I love you, I love you, I love you.

Find a few worship songs that lift your heart. Linger with them, play them over and over, and simply tell Jesus you love him. Put them on your iPod; play them in your car. The more you practice this, the richer it becomes.

When you smell coffee in the morning, say, "Jesus, I love you." When something makes you smile. Over a great bowl of noodles. When you read a passage in a book that moves you, or answers a question. Taking a hot bath. Watching your children play. Walking by a florist shop. When someone is kind. After the rain makes the city lights glisten in the streets downtown. When you hear a piece of music you love. Say, "Jesus, I love you. I love you. I love you."

This doesn't need to be complicated.

Francis of Assisi was called "the second Christ" because his life was so totally given over to expressing the life of Jesus. What can we learn from this man devoted like no other? "As Saint Francis did not love humanity but men, so he did not love Christianity but Christ," wrote Chesterton. Wow. Just let that sink in. Francis didn't fall in love with church; he fell in love with *Jesus*. "His religion was not a thing like a theory but a thing like a love-affair."[1]

Who even remembers him for that? If people know him now it's only as the statue in the garden of the friar with the birds and bunnies. He's been made a cartoon by the religious fog, just as it happened to Jesus. Which brings us back to something essential for loving Jesus, for making your faith more like a love affair—you are going to have to break with the religious. If you want Jesus, you're going to have to end the relationship with the religious glaze.

To begin with, and to help you make a simple practice of loving Jesus, you will find it immensely helpful to be released from false reverence.

It was time for supper.... Jesus knew that the Father had given him authority over everything and that he had come from God and would return to God. So he got up from the table, took off his robe, wrapped a towel around his waist, and poured water into a basin. Then he began to wash the disciples' feet and to wipe them with the towel he had around him. When Jesus came to Simon Peter, Peter said to him, "Lord, are you going to wash my feet?" Jesus replied, "You don't understand now what I am doing, but someday you will." "No," Peter protested, "you will never ever wash my feet!" Jesus replied, "Unless I wash you, you won't belong to me." (JOHN 13:2–8 NLT)

This is a marvelous story. Peter looks Jesus in the face and says, "No!" You've got to love his conviction. Very reverent. Only, it's the wrong application. Peter tries to draw the line at Jesus washing his feet, acting out of good intentions from a sincere respect of his Master. You learn something important about Jesus when he doesn't allow that line to be drawn. He washes his feet anyway. Jesus is *so* iconoclastic. He continues to shatter our stained-glass views of him.

But this motive—reverence for God—is a slippery one. This lets in a great deal of the clutter that gets between us and God, because it *seems* like the proper thing to do.

For example, many Catholics find Mary a more approachable figure, because Jesus has been lifted so far into the heavens he seems altogether gone. Too holy to speak to and, honestly, a bit severe. So they pray to Mary to approach Jesus on their behalf. But when the man with leprosy ran up to him, Jesus didn't insist he come through a mediator. He never did with anyone. This battle with false reverence is not a "Catholic" thing. The morning prayer in the Anglican/ Episcopal Book of Common Prayer begins, "Almighty God and Everlasting Father," a beautiful expression and one I have used many times myself. But *very* different from the one Jesus gave us—Abba. Daddy.

"Papa, I come to you this morning" has a *totally* different feel than "Almighty God and Everlasting Father." Even if you do not start out that way, addressing God with a coat-and-tie formality you would never have wanted between you and your dad will end up starching the relationship. "Papa" is what Jesus gave us. "For you did not receive a spirit that makes you a slave again to fear, but you received the Spirit of sonship. And by him we cry, 'Abba, Father.'... Because you are sons, God sent the Spirit of his Son into our hearts, the Spirit who calls out, 'Abba, Father'" (Rom. 8:15; Gal. 4:6).

In many Protestant circles, Jesus is referred to as "the Good Lord," a phrase that sounds pious, but it's a marshmallow phrase—sweet, spongy, and void of personality. Very white-robe-and-sandals. Jesus never used that term. None of the disciples did. What would happen to your marriage if you only called your wife "the good woman"? Ladies, what would become of your relationship if your husband insisted that you address him as only "Good sir"? How would the dynamics of your relationship with your closest friend change if you were required to no longer use his or her first name, but rather the more formal, "Mr. Smith," or "Miss Jones"?

This is how the religious cleverly separates us from Jesus.

When Saul encounters the risen and ascended Lord on the road to Damascus, he asks him, Who *are* you? "I am Jesus, whom you are persecuting" (Acts 9:5). My name is Jesus. That's pretty straightforward. Not Mr. Christ. We're the ones who keep inserting respectable gold-leafed expressions such as "the Good Lord," "the Savior," "the all-glorious One," feeling better for offering the reverence but not realizing it is religious talk—not the sort of thing Jesus liked very much.

I realize I'm challenging things that good people hold sacred. The point is not the words; the point is the *fruit*, their *effect*. Stained-glass language reflects a view of what Jesus is like; *it shapes our perceptions of him* and, therefore, our experience of him. Whatever the term may be, just ask yourself: *Does this sound like his actual personality? Does this capture his playfulness, infuriating the Pharisees; his humanity, generosity, and scandalous freedom? Does this sound like the Jesus at Cana, at dinner with "sinners," on the beach with the boys?*

Or, does the phrase conjure a more "religious" image of Jesus?

The original writers of the Bible did not use "Thee" and "Thou," didn't even use a capital *H* when referring to "him." We added these later, as an act of reverence. Along with red ink, to set apart the words of Jesus. But the *effect* is to create a very false impression, a best-to-keep-our-distance piety. These ways of speaking about Jesus *perpetuate* distorted views of his personality and keep Jesus at a distance, the polar opposite of the intimacy his entire life was committed to. It makes it hard to love him.

But I can feel the hair rising on the back of the religious spirit even now. Careful, friends—don't let that false piety distort your mood here. This stuff actually gets in the way of loving Jesus. Listen—you can honor him, respect him, insist that others do, and never actually *love* Jesus. This is not what he wanted.

False reverence is a choice veil of the religious fog. It will bring a shroud between your heart and his.

Speaking of veils—the moment Jesus died on the cross, "The curtain of the temple was torn in two from top to bottom" (Mark 15:38). This is an enormously symbolic and staggering event. That curtain existed to separate the rest of the temple from the place called "the Holy of Holies." The presence of God dwelt in that forbidden chamber, while the faithful were kept out. It was a *very* clear message— God was too holy for us to approach. The Jews didn't even dare utter his name.

But we do. We're on a first-name basis. Because Jesus changed everything.

Through his cross he paid for our sin, cleansed us, bought us out of the dungeons of the evil one and brought us back to his Abba. Jesus established a whole new way of relating to God. He often reclined at meals with people; he stopped along the road to chat; he touched them, embraced them. He called them by name, and they him. Jesus is always closing the distance. The encounters in the Gospels are *intimate*. My goodness, the whole incarnation is intimate. Immanuel, God *with* us. Why do we feel we must help Jesus set that mistake right by pushing him off a bit with reverent language and lofty tones? I understand that much of it is done with good intention, by men and women who want to honor Christ. Just like Peter. But the irony is, this isn't how *God* chose to relate to us.

When Jesus died, that most holiest of curtains was ripped in half. Torn, top to bottom. And who was it that did that? Surely not the priests. It was God himself. He took that veil and ripped it in two.

So why do we insist on stitching it back up?

A whole lot of what passes for worship, sacrament, and instruction in Christian circles is sewing lessons—hanging that veil again. Done in the same spirit that says, "God is too holy for us to approach." I've read it countless places, written by popular theologians. I've heard it said many times from the pulpit. We must not be too familiar with God. Do not presume to come too close.

Said who?

They are trying to re-create the Holy of Holies in the name of reverence. Except, it was God who ripped that curtain forever with his own two hands. That is clearly over. Understanding this truth will open up new realms for you in relating to Jesus, and enable your heart to love him.

Think of the woman whose tears poured over Jesus' feet, wiping them with her hair, kissing them. Jesus loved that moment. John was leaning on his chest during the Last Supper. Jesus reached out to touch the leper, the blind man; he held children in his lap. Intimate, intimate, intimate. Do you recall the parable he told about the prodigal son? It says, "But while he was still a long way off, his father saw him and was filled with compassion for him; he ran to his son, threw his arms around him and kissed him" (Luke 15:20). Jesus is explaining how God wants to relate with us. By using the phrase "threw his arms around him and kissed him," he meant that he threw his arms around him and kissed him.

Does this sound like the hymns sung, the prayers said, the way God is approached in your church? I hope so.

Peter learned his lesson, by the way. A week or two after the foot washing, following the cross and the empty tomb, Jesus appears on the shore just across from where the boys are fishing. He acts like a guy out for a stroll, asks if they had any luck, suggests they try one more spot, and reproduces the catch that caught them all in the beginning. Watch how Peter responds this time:

> The disciple whom Jesus loved said to Peter, "It is the Lord!" As soon as Simon Peter heard him say, "It is the Lord," he wrapped his outer garment around him (for he had taken it off) and jumped into the water. (JOHN 21:7)

Peter is a hundred yards offshore. That's about three city blocks—a long way to swim, especially in a full-length robe. It would be like trying to swim wrapped in a bedsheet. Peter doesn't care. He doesn't wait for the boat, forgets about the fish, and as quick as you can say, "Jack be nimble" he hits the water, swimming, thrashing, gasping for air, then stumbling ashore fast as he can to get to Jesus. Do you think he then drew another line in the sand? "Hello, sir. Mr. Christ, may I approach?" Peter is a passionate, emotional, impulsive guy. He just swam a hundred yards in his bathrobe. I'll bet dollars to donuts he ran right up to Jesus, sopping wet as laundry from the washer, and hugged him, soaking the risen Lord.

If Peter didn't do it, you know Jesus did, adding his tears of joy to the wet embrace.

Beautiful. That's the way to do it, friends. Just begin to make a practice of loving Jesus. Relate to him as you see his friends did in the Gospels.

FIRST THINGS FIRST

Now, let me add one last word here that will help you in loving Jesus—doing things *for* God is not the same thing as loving God.

Jesus loves the poor—so, movements have arisen that make service to the poor the main thing. Even though Jesus never said that being poor was more noble or even spiritual. The latest craze is justice—so we rush off to the corners of the globe to fight for justice...and often leave Jesus behind. We actually come to think that service for Jesus *is* friendship with him. That's like a friend who washes your car and cleans your house but never goes anywhere with you—never comes to dinner, never wants to take a walk. But they're a "faithful" friend. Though you never talk.

How many children have said, "My dad worked hard to provide for us—but all I ever really wanted was his love"?

This is—yet again—one more cunning ploy of the religious to keep us from the kind of intimacy with Jesus that will heal our lives. And change the world. We are not meant to merely love his teaching, or his morals, or his kindness or his social reforms. We are meant to love the man himself, know him intimately; keep this as the first and foremost practice of our lives. It is a fact that people most devoted to the work of the Lord actually spend the least amount of time with him. First things first. Love Jesus.

Six days before the Passover, Jesus arrived at Bethany, where Lazarus lived, whom Jesus had raised from the dead. Here a dinner was given in Jesus' honor. Martha served, while Lazarus was among those reclining at the table with him. Then Mary took about a pint of pure nard, an expensive perfume; she poured it on Jesus' feet and wiped his feet with her hair. And the house was filled with the fragrance of the perfume. But one of his disciples, Judas Iscariot, who was later to betray him, objected, "Why wasn't this perfume sold and the money given to the poor? It was worth a year's wages." He did not say this because he cared about the poor but because he was a thief; as keeper of the money bag, he used to help himself to what was put into it. "Leave her alone," Jesus replied. (JOHN 12:1–7)

Another beautiful snapshot of his personality. There is something so humble and gracious about Jesus' ability to receive this. He's been giving, giving, giving—even in his grief and in his weariness he has been giving—and now he lets someone do something for him. Something extravagant and loving. This reveals the beauty of his personality—that he can receive this gift, appreciate it, be grateful for it. He's very moved, and he silences Judas for rebuking her.

The story was recounted for *our* benefit, to help us love him.

"Do I bring something to your heart, Jesus?" You do. Remember Gethsemane? Stay with me—I want you to stay with me. Do not let those religious crows with all their squawking shame you away from this by their false reverence, making you think this diminishes the all-sufficiency of God. Look at Jesus. In the very moment Christ most admits his divinity (allowing himself to be worshipped by Mary), he reveals his desire for intimacy with us.

This is what *Jesus* chose—this is how he acted with his friends. It is the religious who say you can be the kind of Christian Jesus desires *by shunning* this sort of intimacy.

So, I am making a practice of loving Jesus. Loving him for who he really is. The Jesus who gave us the oceans and the rivers. Who gave us laughter. Who served up 908 bottles of wine to Cana. And this one shift has changed my life in ways nothing else can even compare to.

But this is a difficult thing to describe with ink on paper. As Phillip said to Nathanael, come and see.

If you have never given your life to Jesus Christ, now would be the perfect time. This is the moment he chose for you. Time for you to come home to the heart of God. This prayer will help you:

Jesus, I need you. I need your life and your love. I believe you are the Son of God. I believe that your death on the cross was for me—to rescue me from sin and death and to restore me to the Father. I choose right now to surrender my life to you. I turn from my sin and my self-determination and I give my life to you. Thank you for loving me and forgiving me. Come and take your rightful place in my heart and in my life. Be my Savior and my Lord. Live in me; live through me. I am yours.

CHAPTER FOURTEEN

LETTING JESUS BE HIMSELF—WITH YOU

When Jesus spoke to Jolie, she was as surprised as the woman at the well.

Her father was an abusive alcoholic; when she was twelve he told her he didn't want her anymore. "I begged him to love me, to please keep me, but he told me to leave." She was passed through two different adoptions. Sexual abuse occurred, then a trial in which she had to testify. At nineteen she became pregnant out of wedlock. I needn't go on; you understand there was pain and brokenness. Enough to sink a ship. It didn't only shatter her self-image; it also shattered her image of Jesus.

"I had always thought that Jesus went to the cross for all the good people," she wrote, "and that people like me get to be saved because we accept his blanket offer and he's obligated to honor his word." I was nearly weeping to hear her story. And angry—I was getting very angry. I knew where this was coming from. "I didn't think there was any way he would have actually chosen me if he had a choice. I was always afraid that God would discard me if I asked for too much or if I rocked the boat too hard with my sin."

A beautiful woman, a beautiful heart yearning for God, held hostage by sanctified lies for how many years? Can you hear the religious fog behind her words—the way the enemy distorted her view of Jesus and the cross? Sinister, but so convincing because the ideas seemed to exalt Jesus. By crushing her. Wicked, wicked, wicked. And very common.

Jolie wrote me after she attended her first event held by Christian women—something she was very reluctant to do. Understandably. She longed to experience Jesus at the retreat, but she hadn't felt him at all. When it was announced Saturday night that they would be having an extended time of worship, she was disappointed. "My first thoughts were, *This is going to be so boring.* But I began as instructed— I tried to think of myself sitting at Jesus' feet and worshipping him." This is where her story gets really good.

"Suddenly I started to see pictures. I was standing at the foot of the cross."

Whoa. Many of us who love Jesus are brought to tears merely by a reenactment of the crucifixion. A simple cross can stop us in our tracks. Can you imagine seeing the actual event?! Jesus took Jolie there personally.

"He looked down and said, *This is for you.*"

She was simply trying to begin a practice of loving Jesus. It opened her heart to experience him in a pretty dramatic way. He came to her personally, took her in real time to Golgotha. He spoke to her deepest deception, wounding, and fear. *This is for you.* I am speechless—have you ever heard anything more beautiful?

But her story goes on. "The picture changed and I was standing outside the tomb. Jesus emerged and held out his hand and said, 'Come with me.' There was invitation and desire in his eyes. I took his hand and we walked together. He touched my face." Doesn't it remind you of the way Jesus was with the women he loved—with Mary of Bethany, the Samaritan divorcée, and the woman with the alabaster jar, whom Jesus defended in front of a crowd of Pharisees? Invitation and desire in his eyes.

"He told me he had a gift for me. He brought out his hand from behind his back and there was my husband holding his hand. The three of us danced together. We came to a mountain. As we started up, there were places I couldn't get past and my husband helped me, and places he couldn't get past and I helped him. Lastly we came to a place neither of us could pass and Jesus helped us. At the top of the mountain there were lots of people milling about. We looked at Jesus and he simply said, 'Introduce me.'"

What a breathtaking encounter. I want to fall prostrate. I want to run around with my hands over my head, whooping, "He's the same! Jesus is the same—yesterday, today, and forever!"

But some dear hearts are wondering, *Is this sort of thing biblical? Is this real? How come I never experience Jesus like this?*

The test of any report like Jolie's is really quite simple—is it consistent with Scripture, and what is the fruit? She finished her letter by saying, "Jesus showed me clearly that he chose me and that he went to the cross for me. I felt truly, completely loved. He showed me that my husband is a gift from God; that I can trust in his love. This one experience has fundamentally changed my life." I think that speaks for itself.

What if we *could* experience everything we've seen about Jesus in this book? What if that were *available*? Why, then, don't people talk more about this? Where are the encounters with this magnificent Jesus? Permit me to attempt an answer with a parable.

One day a man decided to board himself up inside his house.

He sealed off the doors, the windows, even the chimney. He left only one opening—the kitchen window—through which anyone who wished to speak to him was forced to speak. Fortunately, there *were* people that still wished to speak to him, so they called on the man at his kitchen window.

Over the years this fellow came to the conclusion that the world was such a place in which people only speak to one another through kitchen windows. He wrote a book in which he argued that human discourse cannot and does not take place in any other way than through kitchen windows.

The Kitchen Window School was founded shortly after his death.

Our experience of Jesus is limited most often by the limits *we* put on him! A painful truth, but also a hopeful one. Perhaps we can take down some of those barriers.

Most of the limits we put on Jesus happen unconsciously. Sometimes we place the limits intentionally. And of course, a trainload is dumped on us by our context (in which case the parable could begin, "One day a man was boarded up inside his house by his past," or, "by the leaders of his religious community"). But I'm not looking to fix blame. I'm trying to help us find Jesus. As I said at the beginning of the book, though Jesus has been vandalized by both religion and the world, he is still alive and very much himself. He's still the same beautiful outlaw, with the same personality—though it does require removing some debris nowadays to know him as he truly is.

Step one to a deeper experience of Jesus is knowing what to look for. That's why we have been looking at his personality, setting him free from the religious marshmallow. If you can hang on to this, an entire new world will open up for you. This is a Jesus you can actually love because *this is who he is.*

Step two involves removing some of the debris that has been piled in the way, so that we can begin to experience him, share our lives with him. For example, if you believe, for whatever reason, that "Jesus doesn't speak to me," it's going to be hard to hear him speaking to you. Or believe it *was* him when he does. For the very same reasons, if you hold in your heart that "Jesus doesn't really love me," as poor Jolie did, then it will be awfully hard to experience the love of Jesus. Are you following me?

It is a stunning realization: You will find Jesus pretty much as you expect to.

Not because he *is* exactly as you expect him to be, but because he would be known by you, and you have insisted that he act only within the boundaries you've set. You've insisted he call at the kitchen window. Jesus will accept those terms of engagement for a while—like a loving parent will do with their teenager—because he wants relationship with you. He'll suffer these limits for years. This explains why one denomination experiences Christ in one way, and another denomination experiences him differently. And why both are missing massive portions of his personality. They created rules, outside of which they forbid him to act.

Peter tried this at the Last Supper, when he forbade Jesus to wash his feet. Friends, you don't want to be telling Jesus what he can and can't do. So, the best place to begin and one of the most powerful things you could ever pray is this:

I renounce every limit I have ever placed on Jesus. I renounce every limit I have placed on him in my life. I break all limitations, renounce them, revoke them. Jesus, forgive me for restraining you in my life. I give you full permission to be yourself with me. I ask you for you—for the real you.

You'll probably want to pray that more than once as you go along.

Maybe the most devastating limit is simply the idea that "Jesus doesn't act like that anymore." (Or, "Jesus doesn't act like that with me.") Sure—he was amazing in the Gospels. But that was then and this is now and things have changed. Or so the idea goes. In one fell swoop, this belief shuts down just about everything and anything we could hope to experience with Jesus. It simply slams the door and leaves us standing on one side and him on the other. You wonder if this isn't implied in the famous passage from the book of Revelation where Jesus says, "Here I am! I stand at the door and knock. If anyone hears my voice and opens the door, I will come in and eat with him, and he with me" (3:20).

This takes place later than the Gospel stories, mind you—long after the resurrection and the ascension. It is a letter written to Christians. Jesus is asking for intimacy with us. Who shut that door and left Christ standing in the street? It clearly wasn't Jesus. He's outside, asking us to let him in.

So let him in.

Jesus, come in. I give you total access to every aspect of my life. Come in, Lord. Reveal yourself to me.

We begin to open the door by renouncing the lie that Jesus doesn't act toward us the way he acted toward people in the Gospels.

If we could get a little perspective, we'd see how absurd it is to hold, on the one hand, that the Gospels are the definitive word on Jesus, while holding, on the other, that he doesn't behave like that anymore. God gives us his Son, and grounds the record for all time in the four Gospels. This is who Jesus is. Against all other claims, doctrines, accounts, this is Jesus Christ. But then—as many Christians have been led to believe—God changed the rules. "That's not available to you now." You can't reach out to him in faith as did the woman with the issue of blood and be healed by his life as she was. You can't cry out to him and have him deliver you of a foul spirit. You can't lean upon his breast in intimacy.

It's psychotic.

It's also blasphemy. He is the same, yesterday, today, and forever.

Let's be honest. What is usually going on—what has proven true in every case I have ever encountered—is something more like this: "*I* don't experience Jesus personally, so we must not as a rule be able to experience him personally." Or, "I don't experience Jesus like that (his playfulness, generosity, freedom, intimacy), so he mustn't do *that* anymore." The Kitchen Window school.

But then—what do you do with Jolie's story?

Those who teach that Jesus doesn't act the way he did in the Gospels anymore—and they "teach" it most powerfully by their silence, by never showing others how to experience Jesus like this—these leaders face one embarrassing detail. Jesus is doing it all over the world, in the lives of millions. So the folks who cling to "He doesn't do that anymore" have a real problem on their hands. Either they accept the reality and adjust their theology, or they have to somehow deny millions of experiences.

You shall know them by their fruit. What is the fruit of reports like Jolie's encounter? People drawing closer to God. People coming to faith in Christ. People walking in a fuller experience of his presence. Joy. Love for God. Worship. Adoration. It is a pretty deep religious spirit that dismisses this evidence. May God help them to break with it.

Jesus still acts like himself, he is still Faithful and True, and you can experience him in these very ways. As long as you break agreement with the limits you place on him—like this one.

Honestly, friends, we have been a little naive. We thought knowing God would come easily. We didn't account for the fact that we still live behind enemy lines. If knowing Jesus is the single most important thing that could ever happen to a person, then would it not follow that our enemy would have a very strong investment in keeping this from happening? So he'll throw whatever he can in the way. Here are a few more categories that will help you clear the debris that might be in the way of a deeper encounter with Jesus on a far more regular basis:

OUR OWN BROKENNESS

At the outset of the book I asked, "What do you think of Jesus?" Here is a very revealing way to get at the issue from another angle: What do you think Jesus thinks of *you*?

You discover what you actually believe about Jesus when you admit what it is you believe he thinks of you. Jolie felt that Jesus would never, ever choose her. That she was barely forgiven, tossed into the company of saints because God had to, not because he wanted to. That view of Jesus came out of her brokenness.

A friend of mine holds something lower than a low view of himself. You might say he keeps his self-image in a dark, smelly corner of the basement. He never likes to pass a mirror. He hates it when someone pays him a compliment, and he dismisses it immediately, as proof that you don't really know him. His childhood story is about as heartbreaking as Jolie's, and the self-contempt that got in through that trauma sank its talons deep. It has damaged his relationship with God in many, many ways. Repentance becomes beating himself up. Taking up his cross becomes self-hatred. Shame and self-loathing are what he thinks it means to be humble. The offers of intimacy with Jesus seem too good to be true. "God would never speak to me," he often says.

Over the years his view of God became severe. A gifted teacher, he began to spread his brokenness by convincing others that God was angry, ready to judge, usually impatient with our attempts to love him. Tormented himself, he spread the torment of his misunderstanding. Alas, alas, this is far too common. These folks can grow big churches.

Listen to how someone prays—it will reveal what they really think about Jesus. Does he sound near, or does the prayer make him seem far away, up above the sky somewhere? Does it sound as though Jesus might be someone we are bothering with our requests, someone with far more important things to do? Does he have a sense of humor, or is he always serious? Is it formal, and religious, or "Good morning, Papa"? Do they even sound like they know him? Really, listen to their prayers. Listen to your own.

We interpret Jesus through our brokenness. A painful truth, but also a hopeful truth. Maybe we can open up the doors and windows we didn't know we closed.

For as long as I can remember, I have been haunted by the feeling that "it's never good enough." It doesn't particularly matter what "it" is—it might be a project, a friendship, painting a house, being a father. It's just never good enough. This began way before I met Jesus. It is one of the core pressures I have lived under all my life. No matter what I'm doing, it never feels good enough. Now, I became a Christian with this belief already deeply rooted in my psyche, and what happened was, it got attached to Jesus as well. Nothing ever really feels good enough for him. I'm not doing enough, I'm not loving him enough, I'm not...you get the picture.

This has absolutely nothing to do with who Jesus really is. My brokenness is shaping my experience of him.

This is actually good news, friends—a fair share of your difficulty with Jesus is simply your own brokenness getting in the way. It's good news because it enables us to realize that our perceptions may be wrong, that this isn't what Jesus is like—this is our brokenness talking. And second, healing our brokenness is *exactly* what Jesus came to do. How did he handle every broken person that ever came to him?

The way to begin to get free of this debris, to remove these limits you've unknowingly placed on Jesus, is first to name what the problem is. Where are you having a hard time with Jesus? Where is your struggle with him?

> Do you find it hard to believe he loves you? Or that he loves
> you because of what you do?
> Do you feel like you are always disappointing him?
> Is he mad at you? Ignoring you?
> Does Jesus seem like a hard man who wants you to work
> harder?
> Does he seem distant—loving, sure, but disengaged?

It would help to write this down. What do you think Jesus thinks about you? Then look at what you've written—do you see how this might be connected to your own brokenness? Is this how everyone else feels about you? How you feel about yourself? Ask the Holy Spirit—the Spirit of Truth—to show you how this is connected to your brokenness.

Next, invite Christ into it—invite him right into the whole ugly mess. Open the door, for heaven's sake. The incarnation ought to be proof enough that Jesus doesn't shy away from getting down in the muck of this world. There isn't *anything* you can show him he hasn't seen before. It's not like he's going to be shocked. Or angry. Or disappointed. Jesus *loves* to come; just open the door to him here.

Tell Jesus what you think he thinks of you. Ask him if it's true. Ask him to free your heart from the wounds of your past so that you might know him and love him. This will actually turn out to be a rich part of your learning to love and experience Jesus, this shared journey into and *out of* your brokenness. You'll love him more for it, too. Just as Jolie did.

And Peter, too.

Think back to the story of Jesus and the boys fishing, post resurrection. Remember now—what did Peter do as Jesus was being tried and tortured? He renounced him. Not once, but three times. Then the rooster crowed and Jesus—face swollen, upper lip already burst open and bleeding—looked him right in the eye. Peter ran outside and wept. Can you imagine how torn apart he was inside? How full of shame and self-loathing? The doubt that Jesus would ever want to see him again? When the 153 large fish pop into the nets, and John figures out it's Jesus, Peter hits the water swimming like a Labrador retriever. And there, on the beach, Jesus restores him.

I wouldn't be surprised if he arranged that whole wonderful moment just for Peter.

FORGIVING JESUS

Yesterday morning I was reading my Bible when a note fell out. It was a 3 x 5 card on which a message had been scrawled in a rough hand.

The note was given to me by a complete stranger, at the close of a workshop I recently gave. The man disappeared, and I tucked the note away in my Bible and forgot about it till yesterday. The note said this:

> As I pray for you, I believe Jesus says to you, "My brother, I know the pain that is there and I am here to pull this dart from your heart. The betrayal has been hurtful, but the victory shall be great! I have hands to make all things new!" I had a picture of Jesus holding your heart, removing the dart and healing the wound.

We are known, my friends, we are known. I had no doubt what the "dart" referred to, what the betrayal was. It did not come through friend, nor foe. I felt betrayed by God.

In the past few months I have gone through a great deal of personal suffering. My father is dying. I have had chronic physical pain, as has my wife. One of our sons has been in a terrible emotional trial, the sort of which breaks a parent's heart. Subtly, oh so subtly, what crept in like poison in a wound was a hurt toward God—*Why did you let this happen?*

All but the angel and the Pharisee experience this sooner or later.

As you have been reading this book on the personality of Jesus— his generosity, his playfulness, how amazing he is with others—little doubts have been whispering in the background, *Yes... but.* "But if he is that good, how come..." Finish the sentence. How come he let my dad abuse me and my sister. Let my mother suffer so long with cancer. Didn't stop those terrorists. The objections race forward. It doesn't have to be major crises. Sometimes it is simply the long, slow poisoning of disappointment, frustration, hope deferred.

A slow but steady erosion of what we believe about God takes place. *Yes… but.*

If those "buts" are there, they *will* be a major obstacle to loving Jesus and experiencing him. This is far more common than most people know.

A friend of ours called to ask for prayer. We met, not quite sure what was on the agenda, but willing to help if we could. She said she didn't feel Jesus anymore. Didn't *want* to feel him anymore. Surprising words from a woman who once had a pretty intimate relationship with Jesus. She began to talk about the suffering she and her family had been through—bankruptcy, losing everything, and then church folk blaming them for bringing it on themselves through some unconfessed sin. (Which was not the case—this was during the economic collapse of 2009. Can you see why I hate the religious fog?)

As she opened up the well of suffering in her soul, I could feel the loving, concerned presence of Jesus in the room. With all the intention you see in him toward the woman at the well, or the rich young ruler, I could feel him getting in position to rescue this heart. Rather than jumping to offer encouragement, counsel, or advice, we simply prayed. "Jesus, what are you saying in response to all this?" I heard his loving voice very clearly:

You think I did this.

It was the same strong, kind voice I now see him using all the time in the Gospels, but never saw before because I was watching television with the sound turned off. I had removed his personality from the stories. He said it again:

You think I did this.

Our friend was speechless. The "faithful church girl" part of her heart didn't want to admit what she was really feeling. But pain has a way of stripping all pretense. "Yes, I do," she said.

You need to forgive me.

Now that really blew her away. Forgive God? This idea is going to cause some readers to freak out. Just listen for a moment. If you are holding something in your heart against Jesus—the loss of someone you love, a painful memory from your past, simply the way your life has turned out—if you are holding that against Jesus, well, then, it is between you and Jesus. And no amount of ignoring it or being faithful in other areas of your life is going to make it go away. In order to move forward, you are going to need to forgive Jesus for whatever these things are.

"But Jesus doesn't need our forgiveness!" you protest. I didn't say he did. I said that *you* need to forgive Jesus—you need it.

Let me be clear: To forgive a person, we pardon a wrong done to us; "Forgiving" Jesus means to release the hurt and resentment we hold against him.

This comes *before* understanding. We don't often know why things have happened the way they have in our lives. What we *do* know is that we were hurt, and part of that hurt is toward Jesus, because in our hearts we believe he let it happen. Again, this is not the time for sifting theological nuances, but this is why it is *so* important for you to look at the world the way Jesus did—as a vicious battle with evil. When you understand you have an enemy that has hated your guts ever since you were a child, it will help you not to blame this stuff on God. Anyhow, the facts are it happened, we are hurt that it happened, and part of us believes Jesus should have done something about it *and didn't*. That is why we need to "forgive" him. We do so in order that this part of us can draw near him again, and receive his love.

Perhaps part of the fruit of that restoration will be that Jesus will then be able to explain to us why things happened the way they did. This is often the case. But whether we receive this or not, we know we need Jesus far more than we need understanding. And so we forgive—meaning, we release the offense we feel towards him.

It took her awhile, as is understandable. A long, long silence. Tears. But her love for him allowed her to release it all to Jesus, and almost immediately she began to be aware of his presence again. The e-mails I've gotten from her in the year since are beautiful. "Hey, you're not gonna believe what Jesus just did—this is so cool!" Lots of those stories now.

Restoration. That is our Jesus.

CHAPTER FIFTEEN

CLEARING AWAY THE RELIGIOUS FOG

I actually enjoy it when my wife gets angry. Not at me, of course—though even then it sometimes does make me laugh. Stasi has such a good heart and such a gracious spirit that when she finally does get riled up about something, the moment feels very apropos. Like when she runs the neighborhood bully off from a group of small children. Finally. Go get 'em, girl. It reveals another side of her—a fiery side—and her personality becomes richer, not diminished. The way a person gets angry and what they get angry *about* is a real clue to who they really are.

Wouldn't it get your attention if one of those YouTube videos that goes viral was a clip of Mother Teresa ranting and raging, breaking stuff, yelling at people? You'd watch it, I guarantee it. You would be *fascinated* by her anger because it seems so out of character.

So—what about Jesus? What really fries this gracious, humble, immensely patient man?

Well, the clearing of the temple comes to mind—that's clearly one of those moments where the passion of Jesus breaks out like an avalanche. And what was that all about again? Why was he furious enough to empty the building with the whip he made? Religious falsehood, that's what—religious posing making it hard for people to get to his Father. Justified, sanctified and entrenched—the most difficult kind of barrier to remove, because it is *sanctified*.

There are actually only a handful of accounts of Jesus getting good and mad in the Gospels, which is surprising given how much provocation he was provided. In fact, the specific Greek word for "angry" is used only once to describe him, and where does he happen to be at that moment?

Another time he went into the synagogue, and a man with a shriveled hand was there. Some of them were looking for a reason to accuse Jesus, so they watched him closely to see if he would heal him on the Sabbath. Jesus said to the man with the shriveled hand, "Stand up in front of everyone." Then Jesus asked them, "Which is lawful on the Sabbath: to do good or to do evil, to save life or to kill?" But they remained silent. He looked around at them in anger and, deeply distressed at their stubborn hearts, said to the man, "Stretch out your hand." He stretched it out, and his hand was completely restored. (MARK 3:1–5)

Do you understand why the vast, beautiful heart of Jesus rises in anger toward these clerical bullies? This is the same ferocity we see in the temple. Do you understand the personality of God now, and the horrible nature of religious falsehood? Maybe it is more revealing to ask: Do you *share* his anger at this stuff? This is what infuriates Jesus, so it ought to be what infuriates us. What was the last piece of religious nonsense you were angry with?

Or have you made a cordial détente?

By the way—this is the episode that made those sanctified Stalins so enraged they decided to kill Jesus. For healing a man in church. Because they thought he broke the law. Though the real issue was envy: "It was out of envy that the chief priests had handed Jesus over to [Pilate]" (Mark 15:10). As I said at the outset of this book, if you will simply read the Gospels without bias, you cannot come to any other conclusion but that religion is the enemy—or in the hands of the enemy. Every hostile encounter Jesus has is with very "churchy" people. This spirit is *the* great enemy of our life with God, and it is *this* spirit that Jesus warned his boys about when they were whispering in the boat about the bread: "Be careful," Jesus said to them. "Be on your guard against the yeast of the Pharisees and Sadducees," and then he says it again, to make sure they are paying attention: "Be on your guard against the yeast of the Pharisees and Sadducees" (Matt. 16:6, 11).

If you would know Jesus, love him, experience him, you must pay *very careful attention* to this warning. And friends, you don't heed this simply by making the Pharisees the bad boys of the Bible, like the villains in a melodrama. That is not what Jesus meant. You are already deceived by this stuff if you place the danger "back then, in Bible times."

The religious fog uses sanctified words and activities, things that look and sound very Sunday school to distort our perceptions of God and our experience of him. It is cunning as a snake and adaptive as the flu, infiltrating our practices to make them ever so false. My mom went to Catholic school; it made her walk away from church and God. The fruit of that seems pretty clear. A friend went to seminary, gained a theological degree, and lost his faith. (The inside joke is to call seminary "cemetery." How sick is that?) A good friend was subjected to rigorous Bible classes as a child; she now hates the Bible.

You shall know them by their fruits.

I'm not on a tirade. I want to get on to how we can better love Jesus and experience him. Yet to pass this over would be an injustice to you—this is the source of most of the debris keeping people *from* Jesus. If you want to know him as he really is, to experience him just as intimately as the disciples did, you are going to have to clear out the religious fog.

Now here is my dilemma: There is nothing like a juicy example to make a point clear. But if I name names it will only serve to offend and distract attention from the issue, which is the spirit behind it. Furthermore, that spirit is going to work hard to fog this chapter. So it would be good to pause again and pray what we prayed when we started this adventure:

> *Jesus, show me who you really are. I pray for the true you. I want the real you. I ask you for you. Spirit of God, free me in every way to know Jesus as he really is. Open my eyes to see him. Deliver me from everything false about Jesus and bring me what is true. Deliver me from the spirit of falsehood and everything religious.*

Now, where to begin? It's like trying to find a trick-or-treater on Halloween. Lots of really goofy stuff going on out there in the name of Jesus. But what makes the religious so hard to recognize is that for the most part, people caught up in it are most sincere. Sure—there are always spiritual charlatans and showmen lying through their teeth for power and sex. But most of the time the religious fog is defended and passed along by people of good intent.

So let's start with this point of clarity—there is Christianity, and then there is Christian culture. They are *not* the same. Folks develop a taste for organ music and fog machines in the same way they develop a taste for public radio or NASCAR. Then they insist that organ music or fog machines are *the* way to know Jesus. From here, it just gets weird. Big hair. Reverent tones. Shouting. Robes. Funny hats. Smells and bells. Golden altars. Broadway-style services choreographed down to the second.

And an entire language to go with it.

God is gooood—aaaawllll the tyme. I was drunk in the Spirit. Praise the Lord. Thees and thous, spaketh and wroth. Hallelujah. Did you get the blessing? Having a quiet time. Washed in the blood. Heavenly anointing. Glorious majesty of the eternal mystery. Soaking in the Word. It's too painful to go on. Religious talk is an *immediate* sign of religious infection. But challenge this and folks get mighty defensive.

Loving the *culture* of church is not anywhere close to the same thing as loving *Jesus*. The Pharisees loved their religious culture—the long prayers, the solemn garments, the honor bestowed upon them for being members of the clergy. But they hated Jesus.

In fact—how do folks in your community of faith talk about Jesus? How do they say his name? Does it sound like someone they know, as Peter and Mary knew him? Or is it stuff like Jeeeezus. The good Lawrd. The Good Shepurd. Our eternal Savior. The Christ. I'm not saying we have to refer to him only as "Jesus," but take careful notice of the way his name is said—is it true to his actual personality, or does it sound religious?

Because religious talk is a favorite ploy of the enemy to turn people away from Jesus.

A wing nut talking about Jesus does far more damage than fifty atheists.

How cunning—have people claim something intimate, or powerful with Jesus, but let their lives be so unappealing it ends up having the effect of bad breath. Everybody moves back three paces. You've experienced this, haven't you? "Gifted preachers" who are mean to their children. "Anointed prophets" who cannot sustain ordinary friendship. "Servants of the Lord" who need to be the center of attention, tell you how much their ministry is doing in the world, regale you with amazing stories. The guy whose car is plastered with "Turn or burn" bumper stickers.

Bizarre people are probably the most effective tool of the enemy to turn people off to Jesus. Or, to a more intimate experience of Jesus. The way they talk. The culture they create. But mostly, what they are like to be around. As I have pressed into knowing and loving Jesus more deeply, this is the number one barrier I've had to overcome. Some of the most "spiritual" people I've met, who operate in many powerful gifts, are people I would never want to take on vacation. Would never call at 2:00 a.m. This is a problem, gang. People *loved* to be with Jesus, just be with him in normal life—walking down the road, having dinner, talking on the beach. If your spirituality doesn't "fit" into normal life, it is religious.

Oops—now I *am* gearing up for a tirade.

Here's the test—if you can't take your church culture *and* language and drop it in the middle of a bar or a bus, and have it make winsome sense to the people there, then it's not from Jesus. Because that is exactly what he could do. That's what made him the real deal.

Now, to try to provide an exhaustive list of religious high jinks would require thirty-six volumes or more. Besides, this thing is like the flu—yesterday's witch trial is tomorrow's chapel. What might be more helpful to you would be for me to name some quick test points for you to use.

WHEN THE RELIGIOUS IS OPERATING...

False Reverence Replaces Loving Jesus

In fact, loving Jesus is considered optional. I know, it seems too hard to believe. But it's really quite common. You don't meet a lot of people, frankly, who are given over to loving Jesus. But they live a clean life, attend church faithfully, and are considered to be "good Christians." Good grief—smoking or swearing would draw much more concern than ignoring God in most Christian circles. Do you see the problem here? They're failing at the first and most important command of all—*loving* Jesus. It's as if we think you can be a Christian, but being *in love* with God is optional. Sort of like extra credit.

Question: Is loving Jesus the thing that is given most pulpit time, and most of the casual conversation here? Are most of the people here in love with Jesus? That's pretty straightforward.

Knowing About God Substitutes for Knowing God

Therefore, teaching is exalted. Church feels like a seminar—could be intellectual, could be motivational. Good content is what matters. Doctrine is fiercely defended. Members can explain to you theories of the atonement, or seven steps to success, but can't name one intimate encounter they've had with Jesus. Not once in their lives have they heard him speak to them. I've met heads of Christian education departments, chaplains, and seminary faculty *who by their own admission* don't know Jesus personally. You can talk about sunshine and live your life underground; you can even go to the sea but never dive in. A great deal of what is adamantly taught about Jesus is taught by people who frankly don't know him very well.

Question: Are your leaders close friends of God? People who actually know and experience this Jesus, helping you to know and experience him?

Power Displays Are Confused for Intimacy with Jesus

This can be hard to expose as religious, because at least there are miracles happening. That's the real deal, right? Well—it's a whole lot better than sitting in a pew collecting cobwebs for forty years and never ever witnessing the power of God. But I can give someone a thousand dollars and it doesn't make them my friend. They can keep coming back to me for more, and it doesn't make them my friend. Jesus healed ten guys of leprosy—only one came back to thank him.

Question: Do people chase the next miracle, or do they chase Jesus? They're not the same.

Religious Activity Is Confused with Commitment to Christ

To draw near to God requires a church function of some kind. Church activities are considered more important than any other type of activity. Those who do not engage regularly in religious gatherings are suspect. To question the centrality of church functions immediately places the questioner outside the faithful. Leaders get *very* defensive about church—but to suggest this fact is to incur something along the lines of malice.

Question: How does this differ from Jehovah's Witnesses or Mormonism? They go to church.

Christian Service Substitutes for Friendship with Jesus

Particularly popular in our age of social justice. Fighting for a cause becomes *the* expression of devotion to Jesus. We take our best and brightest saints and ship them off for indentured servitude. Exhausted Christians working for noble causes, but they do not report a daily personal encounter with Jesus. Over time the work itself substitutes for Jesus, and seeking him seems harder than doing more for him. Martha, Martha. Loving Jesus comes first; out of this will flow whatever work in the world he has for us to do. Without this, any work we take on will be impossible to fulfill.

Question: Who's the hero; who is praised? Who is held up as models for serious Christian commitment in your world? "Here is Jeff—he really knows Jesus," or "Here is Jeff—he serves the poor in India."

The Holiness of God Is Taught by Making Him "Unknowable" or Unapproachable

God is spoken of as a mystery so high and lifted up we cannot possibly be friends. The talk may be very intellectual and philosophical; it may be hyperspiritual talk of the heavens; it might be existential "dark night of the soul" stuff. Do you ever hear Jesus talk like this? Of course there are mysteries to God, but Jesus came to make God *known*. He wants to be known. He is known, by millions. This talk of distance and unknowing ushers in a great fog shrouding the way of those who *do* want to know him. It is harmful, not helpful.

Question: Does the effect of it all obscure the humanity of Jesus? Does God sound as near and clear as he came in the incarnation?

Holiness Is Substituted with Rule-Keeping

We don't smoke and we don't chew and we don't go with girls who do. The Pharisees were experts at this. Minding your manners replaces internal holiness—something Jesus was particularly intent on reversing. This results in technical righteousness. Permit an illustration: You are in a parking lot. It is two in the morning. No other cars are present and no human being within five miles. Can you run the stop sign between parking aisles? Of course. The purpose of the sign is protection of life and property. All is protected; you have fulfilled the spirit of the law. Is this distinction between letter and spirit made clear in your church setting?

Question: Is the scandalous freedom of Jesus explained and *encouraged*? What would your group do with the 908 bottles at Cana? With this book, for that matter?

A Trivial Morality Prevails

I once attended a church where the word *hell* was not permitted to be spoken (though it is often spoken in the Bible). Instead, we were to say, "H, E, double toothpicks" (or "double hockey sticks"). This makes holiness downright silly. Jesus called it straining gnats and swallowing camels. I heard a story just this week of a pastoral search committee interviewing final candidates. They asked one qualified fellow, "Do you drink?" "Well, I have an occasional glass of wine with a meal." One of the elders walked up to him, hit him in the chest with a Bible and said, "You better read this, son." That elder can be a controlling, domineering menace and they will tolerate him for years because he can sure run a meeting. But catch him smoking in the parking lot and he's gone by Monday. Friends—pride and arrogance are far more serious issues than swearing; idolatry and unbelief are far more deadly than smoking or drinking. This group is careful to clean the outside of the cup and dish, but inside they're a haunted house. Trivial morality takes the severe beauty of holiness and makes it ridiculous.

Question: What would it take for a person to get fired from your church, Christian school, or ministry? Are the things on their "list" the things you see Jesus upset about?

The System Operates on the Fear of Man

"What good people might think" rules this world. Members toe the line not because they are captured by God, but because they're afraid of what the gossip mill will say if they don't. If you are part of this system, ask yourself, *Do I feel free to be different? To challenge it? To raise questions?* So much of the cultural rah-rah is actually motivated by the fear of man. The religious has gotten hold.

Question: Do people here act like Jesus—meaning, would they confront a Pharisee as a son of hell, break the Sabbath to heal someone, give a wedding nine hundred bottles of wine? If not—why not?

False Humility Is Honored

And other forms of spiritual posturing. A woman told me that when she comes into her morning prayer time it is with the posture of,

"Who am I, a sinner, to come before you, a holy God?" (She was holding her hands above her head as if to shield herself from a deserved wrath.) Sounds holy. It's disgusting. You don't see a whiff of this in those who *knew* they were the lowest—the woman who anoints Jesus, the leper, Peter after renouncing him three times. They come running to Jesus. False humility is religious.

Question: What sort of humility is modeled in your circle?

There Is Safety in Distance

One more thing about the false reverence—there is a *function* to it that would be good to admit. On the one hand, our soul cries out for Jesus. We yearn (often without knowing what it is we are yearning for) for his life in us, his love, his nearness. On a conscious level, we ache for his comfort, his counsel, his friendship, even for one simple word of affirmation.

On the other hand, we keep a safe distance. He is so true, to be near him is unsettling because it reveals in a general sense all that is not true in us. Sometimes in a very specific sense. It doesn't happen in a barrage; he is too gracious for that. It doesn't always begin with perfect clarity. We are simply unsettled by his presence, as I imagine I might feel in the presence of a silverback gorilla, as a cat is unsettled by the presence of a very large dog. So we pull back.

This is why we accept the false reverence—it's like having a relationship with someone out of state. It doesn't intrude into your life like a spouse or a good friend does. There is safety in the distance. We secure ourselves against a fuller experience of Jesus' presence because he is so unnerving. There is no faking it in the presence of Jesus; there is no way we can cling to our idols and agendas. We sense this intuitively, and so we keep our distance without really *looking* like we're keeping our distance. By using false reverence. "The Good Lord" probably isn't going to show up at your New Year's Eve party.

So, when it comes to experiencing more of Jesus in your life, much depends on what we are *open* to experiencing—what we have been told we can experience, *and*, what we are comfortable with. Are you willing to let Jesus be himself with you?

Now, I think most Christians would agree with what I have said here. But it is remarkable how pernicious religion can be. It sneaks back in, even into the most well-intended operations. (By the way— if you want to understand church history, simply understand the power and intensity of the religious spirit.) Counterfeit currency ruining the economy. Some of you will be set free simply by recognizing it; others will need to pray against the religious fog very intentionally. Those who lead churches and ministries will want to pray regularly to prevent it from infiltrating your efforts.

Now here is a tough pill to swallow. In the Gospel of Matthew Jesus has thirty-four intimate encounters with an individual— "intimate" defined as when someone in particular is singled out for mention, or receives a word or touch from Jesus, or Jesus receives a word or touch from them. Of the thirty-four, one takes place in church. In the shorter Gospel of Mark, there are twenty-six such encounters recorded; two take place at church.

Furthermore, all of the most "famous" stories about Jesus—his birth, baptism, trial in the desert, calling of his disciples, turning water into wine, raising the dead, transfiguration, walking on water, feeding of the five thousand, Sermon on the Mount, calming the storm, Last Supper, dark night in Gethsemane, crucifixion and resurrection—not one of them takes place in church. Not one. This is no coincidence. Jesus came to the most religious people on earth, and much of what he had to do in order to bring them to God was to free them from their religion.

Some of my readers are really going to get their shorts in a bunch over this. (Those of you having the hardest time with this, notice—do you not consider yourself a religious person?) Let me be clear: This is not an antichurch statement. I am not "antichurch." I believe we need worship, sacrament, instruction, community, and service. I go to church. I encourage you to. But you must stick to the facts—one of the most striking aspects of the stories of Jesus told in the Gospels is how few, how *very* few of the events related by the stories take place within a religious setting. The fact is, if you wanted an intimate encounter with Jesus, you would have been far more likely to find it outside church.

This is still true today.

For heaven's sake—there are 168 hours in your week. Are you really going to say that the one or two you spend at church are more important to God than the other 166? That's religious spirit stuff. The spiritual life is meant to be lived out in everyday life. In this sense, Jesus was a very spiritual man, but *never* a religious one.

> This is what is still so hard to believe. It is hard to believe that this marvelous work of salvation is presently taking place in our neighborhoods, in our families, in our governments, in our schools and businesses, in our hospitals, on the roads we drive and down the corridors we walk, among people whose names we know. The ordinariness of Jesus was a huge roadblock to belief in his identity and work in the "days of his flesh." It is still a roadblock.[1]

We should expect Jesus everywhere, anytime.

Furthermore, when church actually inoculates people to a true experience of Jesus—or to an experience of the true Jesus—then yes,

I am *very* anti that sort of church. All the men and women I've met who have spent *decades* in church and still do not know God. If the people you loved came down with cancer, and were told to faithfully attend a center for recovery but at the end of ten years were no better, wouldn't you be mad about that? Wouldn't you at least say that it's time to look for a different clinic?

> The merry bells ring out, the people kneel;
> Up goes the man of God before the crowd;
> With voice of honey and with eyes of steel
> He drones your humble gospel to the proud.
> Nobody listens. Less than the wind that blows
> Are all your words to us you died to save.
> O Prince of Peace! O Sharon's dewy Rose!
> How mute you lie within your vaulted grave.
> The stone the angel rolled away with tears
> Is back upon your mouth these thousand years.[2]

The simple test is this: Do you encounter Jesus in church—or in any of the Christian things you do? Are you drawn into a genuine understanding and experience of Jesus *as we find him in the Gospels*? If not, there's a problem. Don't forget—Jesus healed a man on the Sabbath. The religious leaders decided to kill him. This spirit is mighty nasty—and slippery as an oyster.

Friends, if you would know Jesus as he is, if you would let him simply be himself with you, then run—run as fast as your two feet will carry you from anything that smacks of religion.

CHAPTER SIXTEEN

LETTING JESUS BE HIMSELF—ENCOUNTERS

In 1954 Roger Bannister ran a mile in under four minutes. The world was stunned. No one had ever done that before. Ten years later, Jim Ryun did it in high school. Nowadays a four-minute mile is considered a must if you would be a professional middle-distance runner. Is this simply the result of better shoes? More scientific vitamins?

What happened is that Bannister broke a barrier. Prior to his feat, folks simply didn't know or didn't believe it was possible. Once they saw it *could* happen, many rushed to try to make it happen for themselves.

That is what I want to try to do here—I want to open up the possibilities of experiencing Jesus.

Jolie was utterly surprised when Jesus actually showed up during her time of worship (Why are we surprised he comes, especially in worship?!). When he took her to the cross, she had never experienced *anything* like that before. But actually, this sort of thing is common down through church history. (For Jesus is the same, yesterday, today, and forever.) As I read her story, I was reminded of a very famous moment in the life of Francis of Assisi, when he, too, was given a vision of Jesus on the cross during a time of prayer. It, too, changed his life forever.

Many readers will be familiar with Saint Augustine, a man whose appeal spans Protestant, Catholic, and Orthodox faiths. He was quite an accomplished sinner, by his own admission, a man we would send to a recovery center for sexual addictions. Though he had the opportunity to sit under the preaching of Ambrose, and though his own mother was praying night and day—a most effective weapon for turning a wayward soul—he was bound to his darkness. "I was in torment," he wrote. Until that fateful day when in a garden, he heard God speak—through the voice of a child over a wall:

> Somehow I flung myself down beneath a fig tree and gave way to the tears which now streamed from my eyes, the sacrifice that is acceptable to you.... For I felt that I was still the captive of my sins, and in my misery I kept crying, "How long shall I go on saying, 'tomorrow, tomorrow'? Why not now? Why not make an end of my ugly sins at this moment?" I was asking myself these questions, weeping all the while with the most bitter sorrow in my heart, when all at once I heard the singsong voice of a child in a nearby house. Whether it was the voice of a boy or a girl I cannot say, but again and again it repeated the refrain "Take it and read, take it and read." At this I looked up, thinking hard whether there was any kind of game in which children used to chant words like these, but I could not remember ever hearing them before. I stemmed my flood of tears and

stood up, telling myself that this could only be a divine command to open my book of Scripture and read the first passage
on which my eyes should fall.[1]

He does. They are the very words he needed to hear from God.
And in that moment, which would end up echoing throughout the
world, "You converted me to yourself." Take it and read, or take up
and read, depending on the translator. *Tolle lege* in the Latin. I think
we've missed the playfulness of this. Augustine is a voracious reader.
Books are his language. Jesus—who sent the fisherman fishing and
the tax collector to hand out charity—tells Augustine to get up and
read. Open the book, you bookworm. Through the singsong chant of
a child, which adds an even more playful touch. Jesus was singing his
tune.

Speaking of tunes, I got an e-mail recently from a friend who is a
little embarrassed about his taste in music. While others listen to
Christian stations, he prefers the "New Age Jazz" stuff (not New Age
teaching, an instrumental form of jazz music):

At times I've felt a little odd and maybe even guilty listening to
this genre. But as I was walking out to my car from a particularly difficult sales call, I was asking Him to give me peace and
rest. I asked if He minded that I listened to this station. As I got
in the car, I sensed Him saying, *Oh no, that's fine, I'm here, too.*
I started the car, punched in my station, and on came an instrumental of, "Fairest Lord Jesus." I said, laughing, "Ah, so You are
here!"

I hope that's a common occurrence for you, friends. I've had Jesus
say something to me and the very next moment what he said is

repeated in a song or a movie or from the mouth of a friend. We should expect to encounter Jesus anytime, anywhere, everywhere. The song of a child, a song on the radio—Jesus is infinitely creative. Just let him be himself with you.

Another friend, Leslie, was traveling in Germany and had the privilege of seeing the renowned Oberammergau Passion Play. "All the villagers play parts in the story," she explained. "For nine years they are woodcarvers and then the tenth they take on a whole new part; the men grow beards and let their hair get long." The play is three hours in the morning, followed by a long break, and then it continues in the afternoon. She wrote this account to me:

> During my break I spent quite a bit of time in one particular shop. The woodcarver himself gave me a detailed explanation of his carvings. He had a head full of long brown hair and some woman asked him if he was in the play. "Yes," he replied. I thought, *To whom am I speaking??? Peter, James, John, Judas... Jesus?!* The moment I thought his name it was as if the Lord was saying to me, *You recognize me on the stage in the part you know so well, but do you recognize me in the shop? Have you so compartmentalized your life between sacred and secular, church and business, Sunday and the rest of the week that when I am out there you no longer recognize me?* I realized at that moment that I could walk into church on Sunday and know what to expect because I know the story. I could see Jesus in that setting. Then I would leave and go out into my own world and leave him in first-century Palestine. I couldn't recognize him in the shop.

Jesus is everywhere.

But let me give you a grace that will help you see him:

He said to them, "Therefore every teacher of the law who has been instructed about the kingdom of heaven is like the owner of a house who brings out of his storeroom new treasures as well as old." (MATTHEW 13:52)

This is such a beautiful, gracious, and *stabilizing* verse. It is immensely kind; it is also immensely cunning. So very like Jesus.

Think of it—Jesus was shaking some of his listeners' most cherished assumptions, while inviting them into *very* new ways of understanding God. The veil was coming down—forever. It was a moment ripe for diminishment. Or defensiveness. He moved quickly to dismantle the overreactions. On one hand, some of those present are leaping to, *All these years I have been wrong?!* (It will help to add a Jewish accent.) *So much time in Hebrew school and for what? I am such a schmutz.* They throw ashes on their heads, toss their tallith in the ash can. Diminishment. Certain personalities tend this direction. I know I can.

For years, whenever I'd hear one of those dramatic stories reported by missionaries—the ones where Jesus appears in the midst of a kidnapping or attempted execution, blinds the group of machete-wielding rebels and the would-be martyr walks out unharmed, then leads the village to Christ and becomes best friends with the witchdoctor—I would think to myself, *Geez. I'm such a loser when it comes to Jesus. I don't have anything like that to share. That's the real stuff. I'm playing with blocks on the kindergarten floor.* Something I *haven't* experienced eclipses all that I *have* known of God. Jesus is trying to prevent that plunge into diminishment by saying that our "old" treasures *are* treasures.

On the other hand, Jesus knows he is also dealing with personalities who will fight to the death for what their fathers believed. Those types are at this moment racing to conclusions: *Abraham, Isaac, and Jacob!! This is too much. I will not abandon all my fathers have taught. We must reject this man and his teaching*, they decide, their eyes scanning the ground for stones. This crowd can get ugly in a flash. You know the type. To be honest, most of us have this type in us as well.

In a one-sentence parable Jesus rescues them both. Rescues us.

Don't let someone else's remarkable encounter with Jesus diminish the beauty of what you know of him. Hold fast to the treasures you have.

But, at the same time, you haven't experienced all there is with God. There is more. Much more. Those new possibilities are often opened to us through hearing the ways Jesus is working in other people's lives. Put down both the ashes and the stones. Let's discover more of Jesus, together.

It had been several years since I had seen David, and as he walked into my office yesterday afternoon I was immediately struck by how much he had changed. No, that's not quite right. I was struck not so much by how he had changed, but by how much less of himself he was. He did not seem *different* so much as he seemed *diminished*—as soldiers returning from war often appear. He told the story of his life over these absent years; it was a sad story, filled with disappointments, setbacks, and a loss of heart. But sadder than these was the loss of his friendship with Jesus.

David had come to see me years before as a sophomore in college. His father had died in a swimming accident, and David was reeling from the loss. I now realize that much of what I lumped at the time under the banner of "grief" was in fact a collection of other factors predating the accident, factors I would draw together now under the description of "depression, brokenness, and oppression." Far earlier than his father's death, the young man had lost heart. And come under a cloud of religious veils.

The campus ministry David had joined shortly after coming to Christ was—sadly—deeply infected with the religious. They did not teach the availability of an intimate relationship with Jesus. Focus was on consistent Bible study, witnessing, good morals. Motivation was largely pressure and guilt. A kind of Christian Islam. The fruit was that most of its disciples did not experience Jesus, did not believe in anything supernatural, and lived under a cloud of pressure and guilt. David and I began our time by bringing the cross of Christ between him and that ministry, and all religious oppression that came to him through it. For by the Cross we are crucified to the world and the world to us (see Gal. 6:14).

David summarized his current state of being as, *Why bother? Take the easy road out.* A daily experience of passivity and resignation. I wasn't even sure how we arrived at the moment (but thank you, Holy Spirit) when David began telling me about a day in middle school. "My brother was really good at math and science, so the teacher liked him. I wanted the teacher to like me, too." (David followed his brother in school by two years.) "So I remember I studied really hard for the test. But I got an F. After class the teacher called me up. I was hoping he was going to offer to tutor me. But he just said, 'It's obvious your brother got the brains in the family and you got the looks.' I don't remember what he said from that point on. I just wanted to run from the room."

"What did you feel?" I asked.

"Shame. Terror," he replied.

Jackpot, I thought to myself. *This is clearly one of the ways this darkness got in.* I was especially concerned about his description of how at that moment he no longer heard what the teacher was saying, how reeling under shame and terror of further exposure he simply wanted to run from the room. This sounded like dissociation to me—common for such moments, but deeply concerning. It is not good for the soul to separate from itself; these dissociative moments are ripe opportunities for the enemy to establish a spiritual stronghold. I asked David, "How much would you say you live under a sense of shame?" He didn't even have to pause and reflect: "All the time. Constantly."

We invited Christ into the memory. This was difficult, and risky, because David had lost so much of his relationship with Jesus by this point. "Jesus, come into this memory," we prayed. I waited a moment, and then asked David, "Do you see yourself back in the classroom that day?" "Oh yes." "Is Jesus with you?" "Yes. He is standing between me and the teacher." "Is he facing you, or the teacher?" I asked this because sometimes Jesus will deal with the perpetrator of the wounding first, then turn to the victim. "He has his back to the teacher and he's facing me. It's like he is shielding me from him." *Good*, I thought; *this is good.* Just like Jesus shielding the leper, or Mary, or many others.

"Let's ask Jesus to reveal to you any agreements you made that day." Immediately I heard, *Why bother trying if this is what happens?* I shared that, and David said, "Oh yeah. Also, *I'm so f-ing stupid.*" We prayed for David to renounce those agreements, and also renounce every claim they had given the enemy in his life. "Now, I want you to ask Jesus to take you out of this memory, free you from it," which he did. "Where are you now?" Up till this point—from the moment he stepped into my office—David had been using a very "checked-out" tone of voice, monotone, with a dash of cynicism. Suddenly his voice was alive. He sounded like himself. "We're on a field I used to play soccer on. I loved being there!" "What are you doing?" David was now quietly crying. "We are kicking a soccer ball around."

David left my office that day more hopeful, lighter, with a sense of drawing closer again to Jesus than he had experienced for years. In the collective witness of the church, there are millions of similar encounters. I have been present to hundreds personally, and over the years heard testimony of more than a thousand. Two things are true of every one of these encounters: Jesus' *personality* in them is utterly consistent with what we've discovered in the Gospels, and the fruit is a deeper love of Jesus *because of* the encounter with his personality.

By their fruit you shall know them.

Now, I recognize David's experience may sound strange, or unfamiliar, perhaps unbiblical. So let us bring good theology into this immediately. This is a treasure too many people have had kept from them—either because they did not know it is available, or, through religion masking as "theological concerns."

First, where does Jesus Christ now reside, in the life of the believer? *Inside* us; more precisely, in our *hearts*: "For this reason I kneel before the Father, from whom his whole family in heaven and on earth derives its name. I pray that out of his glorious riches he may strengthen you with power through his Spirit in your inner being, so that Christ may dwell in your hearts through faith" (Eph. 3:14–17). So we should expect to experience Christ *within* us, as well as "with us," or alongside us.

Next, is there any aspect of our personal history that is beyond the reach of Jesus Christ? Never. "All the days ordained for me were written in your book before one of them came to be" (Ps. 139:16). Would the faculty of our memory be a realm beyond the understanding of Jesus Christ, or—more important—beyond his access? No. "Nothing in all creation is hidden from God's sight. Everything is uncovered and laid bare before the eyes of him to whom we must give account" (Heb. 4:13). So, Jesus within us is also Lord of our memory.

Finally, if our relationship with Christ or our witness for him in this world is being hindered because a part of our soul is not yet fully under his loving rule, would Jesus want to address that? Of course he would. Remember his fierce intention.

I have had similar encounters with Jesus in healing prayer. Last year, as a wise old sage was praying with me through some of the painful memories of my life, I was immediately reminded of the time in middle school when my first girlfriend broke my heart. These wounds can linger for a lifetime if you let them—the first cut is the deepest, and all that. We asked Jesus to take me back to the memory. I saw us, the girl and me; it was that fateful summer day. We were in the living room, just as it happened. Then I saw Jesus enter the room. He was quite stern with her, and it surprised me. *That mattered to you?* I wondered. *Very much*, he said.

Then Jesus turned to me. I felt his love. I realized I could let the whole thing go. It was so healing. To understand that Jesus is angry about what happened to you is very, very important in understanding his personality but also in your relationship with him and for your healing. What I love about these encounters is that every time— every time—Jesus is so true to his real personality. Sometimes fierce, sometimes gentle, always generous, and often very playful.

My son was having a tough freshman year at college. So many students there are bound under the religious fog. It was a lonely fall, filled with misunderstanding. One afternoon, just after a classmate said something particularly hurtful to him, Blaine returned to his room and slumped onto his bed, about as low as a young man can get. He looked over to his desk, and "saw" Jesus sitting there, in his desk chair, a smile on his face. He was wearing a pirate hat. Then he disappeared. A whiff of the Emmaus road.

Now, experiencing Jesus doesn't have to be dramatic. Sometimes it is, but not always. When you think of all those days the disciples spent with Jesus, just walking here and there or reclining at the table, the "big-time" miracles actually account for a small portion of those three years. There was just a lot of ordinary living. Jesus comes here, too. In a tulip, a smile, a cup of coffee, the night sky.

Last night I had a horrible night. I don't quite know how to describe it, but if I even use the word *Gethsemane*, I lose all by trying to establish a connection. Hours of evil attack, the fruit of which was, I couldn't find Jesus this morning. I felt as though he had abandoned me. Kneeling facedown in my office, worshipping, my face to the floor, I suddenly felt a presence next to me; something dropped by my ear. It was an old chewed-up toy. I looked and there was Oban, wagging his tail. *Wanna play?* The playfulness of Jesus, cheering my heart through my dog. Oban lay down in front of me, and began to lick my hand. It was so merciful, so comforting; the comfort of Jesus.

If we will get rid of the limits and the religious constraints, we will see him everywhere.

> I see his blood upon the rose
> And in the stars the glory of his eyes,
> His body gleams amid eternal snows,
> His tears fall from the skies.
>
> I see his face in every flower;
> The thunder and the singing of the birds
> Are but his voice—and carven by his power
> Rocks are his written words.
>
> All pathways by his feet are worn,
> His strong heart stirs the ever-beating sea,
> His crown of thorns is twined with every thorn,
> His cross is every tree.[2]

Our dear friend Kim is a missionary in Thailand. As a single woman, it has been a tough several years for her. She doubts it will be possible to meet a good man in the place where she serves. But, over the past few months, she has begun a relationship with a man back home. Mostly, they have to use the Internet. Here's where her story picks up:

It was a Saturday morning and I was enjoying a delicious conversation. I looked at my watch and realized I needed to go meet up with a friend of mine, to take her to a women's event at church. She doesn't know Jesus yet but is hungry. I anticipated lame conversation gorging myself on empty carbs. But I had told her I would go. She was taking a risk and I needed to receive her heart well. So I hung up, grabbed a cab, and headed downtown. Our plan was to meet at the station at 8:45. The minutes rolled on. 9:00. 9:15. 9:25. I imagined walking into the brunch late, plates empty, women looking at us trying to scrounge a seat and some leftovers. I stood there, hundreds of people passing me by with every arriving train. My blood started to boil, growing ever-more frustrated at how I could be at home enjoying conversation with someone I'm coming to care for quite deeply. But instead, I was standing in a fume-filled, sweaty, rumbling train station waiting for a friend who I knew would be late.

In that moment, I heard the voice of Jesus as clear as anything. *So you left intimacy in order to come be disappointed by someone who needed love, huh?* He didn't have to say any more. There was no condemnation in his voice, only that of a kind friend who was letting me into a bit more of his own story. What his humanity was like, what his time on earth must have so often felt like. It made me love him all the more.

When we recover the humanity of Jesus, it helps us find him in the messy parts of our own humanity, of humanity at large. We discover for ourselves the vast richness and beauty of his heart. If his heart is such, in whose image we are made and are being remade, might our own hearts one day be so rich? Which makes me think of another beautiful story, told by our "adopted daughter," Julie. Jesus came to her during a time of prayer. This is what she saw:

We were in a lush and verdant meadow surrounded by oaks and filled with tall grass and wildflowers. Jesus took my hand and led me through the swaying grasses and into a dense wood. Light flickered down through the branches and we laughed and had such fun as I followed him deeper into the woods. We stopped when we came to a giant tree and under thick branches he told me what I needed to hear most: *You are mine.* (I was surprised that this was what I needed to hear most.) As I looked into his eyes I saw the same eyes as my husband and I was able to believe Jesus and receive all of the love he had for me. He took me by the hand again and led me deeper into the forest until we came to a dark low cave. I could see the most amazing array of jewels encrusting the walls of the cave—rubies, diamonds, sapphires, and especially emeralds. I exclaimed that it was so beautiful. He said, *Julie, this is your heart.*

Pause. You will miss the staggering gift of this story if you do not understand that God makes our hearts new. The religious fog has many, many Christians trapped in the Old Testament view of their hearts—deceitful and wicked. They have been blinded to the New Testament teaching that God gives us a new heart: "The seed on good soil stands for those with a noble and good heart," and

"He purified their hearts by faith" (Luke 8:15; Acts 15:9). That'll rock your world.

Julie continues:

We moved out of the cave and back into the forest and he asked me what question I most needed to ask. I asked if I would be a good mom. He gave me a picture of a little blond girl running with a toothy smile (she had two white barrettes in her hair) and as she ran I had my head thrown back with laughter and delight. I am so undone at this and have tears streaming down my face.

Julie will give birth to a little girl by the time this book is published. She didn't know that when Jesus gave her this picture.

Oh, Jesus—why do we doubt you so? Why do we place so many limits on you? Forgive us. I share these stories in hopes that they will enable you to experience Jesus in new ways yourself, give you eyes to see the ways he is already coming for you. Would you like to see his eyes? His smile? Ask him! Let Jesus be who he is with you. Take off the limits you or others have put on him. Oh—one more thing. You need to be open to the ways Jesus *wants* to come to you. Don't insist it be in exactly the way he comes to someone else. This artist is infinitely creative.

My eldest son went through about a nearly two-year depression, though I am sorry to say none of us recognized it for such. Last summer, late at night, he was watching a movie with a friend. It was a story about a young man in depression, and the pain of watching an image of himself lanced Sam's heart. He ran outside; he ran down the street. With tears he begged God to come to him. *Jesus, if you're real, come, right now.* At that moment, that exact moment, three things happened. A bolt of lightning flashed above; his phone rang, a friend four states away was concerned; and he heard footsteps racing down the street to find him (the friend he watched the movie with). "I was kind of hoping, you know, for Jesus to appear bodily. But, this was pretty awesome still."

Let him be himself, friends. He'll come. He'll come.

I was going to call this book *Jesus of a Thousand Hearts*, because of the way he continually breaks into my life. He "speaks" to me through hearts. I'll find stones in the shape of hearts in rivers where I'm fishing. I've seen them almost step-by-step up a mountainside when on a grueling climb. Praying in the morning I'll look out the window and passing by will be a heart-shaped cloud. Dinner rolls, seashells, stains on my jeans. I've won the lottery when it comes to hearts from Jesus. But I am ashamed to admit that last summer, I grew a little impatient with them. I was going through a trying time and seeking God for the answer to many questions. Often, he would simply give me a heart in reply. I'd be walking down the sidewalk, and there in the cement see a heart-shaped hole, made by a bubble when they poured the sidewalk.

I actually grew a little dismissive of them. I didn't want hearts—I wanted *answers*.

So, Jesus stopped giving these treasures of our friendship.

Last fall, while walking through an alpine meadow bow hunting, I was asking him, *How come you don't give me hearts anymore?* I asked it in a pouting kind of way. At that moment something gray caught my eye. I looked down midstride, and there in the grass, about as big as a dinner plate, was a dried piece of cow manure—in the perfect shape of a heart.

If I didn't know Jesus adores me, if I didn't know he is playful, and if our relationship didn't allow me to receive a playful tease, I might have misinterpreted the icon. But I loved it. It was both, *Oh, so now you want a heart?* and, *I adore you still.* A cow-pie heart. That is *so* Jesus. Wish I'd taken a photo of it—we could have put it on the cover of this book.

CHAPTER SEVENTEEN

LETTING HIS LIFE
FILL YOURS

If you were to choose one word to describe the movement of Jesus through those three stunning years of public action we find in the Gospels, what word would it be?

Now, I know, I know—everybody's going to choose the word *love*. But I didn't ask what word you would use to describe his character, his *motives*. I asked what word you would use to describe his presence, the quality of the many diverse actions you see. A mother singing lullabies to her child is moved by love, but her actions are best described as *tender* or *adoring*. A mountaineer struggling forward at twenty thousand feet, exhausted, breathing labored but refusing to give in, is best described as *unrelenting*.

How would you describe the quality of the presence and actions of Jesus? In just chapter 9 of Matthew, this is what we see:

He steps off the boat from rebuking Legion and heals a paralyzed man.

He calls Matthew to join him, has dinner in his home with a scandalous crowd, and rebukes the Pharisees for getting in a snit over it.

He explains why his disciples don't fast—thus opening up the freedom he came to bring.

He raises a little girl from the dead.

He heals two blind men.

Then heals a mute by casting out a demon.

Then journeys through "all the towns and villages" (v. 35), spreading the news about the kingdom of God.

All this, may I remind you, in one chapter. If any of us accomplished this in a decade or a lifetime, we'd be deeply satisfied.

The word I choose to describe Jesus is *life*. Pure, lush, exuberant Life. Life that proves to be unquenchable, unstoppable, indestructible. As John summarized the whole affair, "In him was life, and that light was the light of men" (1:4). It sure was.

Let's turn back to nature one more time. It is *such* a liberating force from the religious fog, because it is God's and it speaks volumes about his true—pardon the pun—nature. What does creation say about his life? A single tree is enough to make me worship—the beauty, the elegance, the perseverance, the life coursing through it. If I were given a lifetime, I could never make one myself. Now—have you ever stopped to imagine how many trees there are on this planet? The Taiga forest spans the globe through Sweden, Siberia, Alaska and Canada. It contains one-third of all the trees on earth and produces enough oxygen to replenish earth's supply.[1] That's one forest.

Have you ever wondered how many fish are swimming our oceans and seas? About seven hundred billion sardines are harvested each year off the coast of Peru—that is one tiny subspecies, off one coastline. There are a lot of fish finning around out there. It boggles the imagination.

Come closer, take a microscopic view of our world. There are hundreds to thousands of organisms in a single drop of pond water—protozoans, amoebas, rotifers, water bears. One drop. How many drops fill a bucket, how many buckets a pond? And there's a lot of ponds on this planet. The earth is like a massive petri dish, teeming and trumpeting with life in such staggering diversity and abundance that science still hasn't come close to cataloging it all.

Nature is bursting with life—even *after* all these years of war.

Now, what would happen if this sort of life expressed itself in a man? Exactly. It did.

When Jesus fed the five thousand, the tally counted only men. So the crowd was probably more like ten thousand including women and children. From fives loaves and two (small) fish. With leftovers. He doesn't even say anything in Cana after, "Fill the jars." The 180 gallons of wine are suddenly just...there. With a shout he raises Lazarus from the dead. One word best describes what is going on here: *life*. Jesus really is the Lord of Life.

Now for a wonder of wonders—not only do you get Jesus, you get to live his life. Really. Everything you've seen here, everything you've read about, this life is yours for the asking. That is what Jesus believed. That was his understanding of our desperation and his mission:

I tell you the truth, unless a kernel of wheat falls to the ground and dies, it remains only a single seed. But if it dies, it produces many seeds. (JOHN 12:24)

I am the vine; you are the branches. If a man remains in me and I in him, he will bear much fruit; apart from me you can do nothing. (JOHN 15:5)

I am the bread of life...the living bread that came down from heaven....Unless you eat the flesh of the Son of Man and drink his blood, you have no life in you. (JOHN 6:48, 51, 53)

I have come that they may have life, and have it to the full. (JOHN 10:10)

The illustrations would have been visceral for his listeners. If they didn't do it themselves, they saw their uncle or neighbor scatter seed every spring; no seed planted meant barren ground. And famine. Vineyards surrounded them, not as charming tourism but as life-blood; they knew any branch broken off withered and died. The branch gets its life from the vine. Bread was their daily subsistence, the staple of their diet. No bread meant starvation.

How do we bring this home to an audience that is utterly discon-nected from the earth?

Think electricity—if you cut the wires leading to your home, you have no power. Think gasoline—if you run out of fuel, your car stops dead in its tracks. This is the point he is trying to make. Better still, think of oxygen—it is one thing to have oxygen around you; it is another thing altogether to have it *in* you. Though you live every day of your life surrounded by it, swimming through a sea of air, if it remains outside you rather than in you, you will die.

And so it is with Jesus, with his life. He is the missing essence of our existence. We need Jesus like we need oxygen.

Aren't you desperate for life? "We are vessels of life," says

MacDonald, "not yet full of the wine of life; where the wine does not yet reach, there the clay cracks, and aches, and is distressed....Life must be assisted, upheld, comforted, every part, with Life. Life is the law, the food, the necessity of life. Life is everything."[2]

It sure is.

Two Reactions

There seem to be two basic reactions when sincere folk encounter the beautiful, scandalous life of Jesus: *I can't possibly do that*, or, *I want to try to live like him*. Both groups fit nicely into our present cultural milieu.

The first camp may not be any less committed to Jesus than the second, but they share a common internal reaction to his life that essentially goes like this: *Well, sure, c'mon—we're talking Jesus here. Of course he was amazing. I can't hope to live like that—so, why even try?* Their posture fits well in a time of self-doubt posing as humility; it can even feel noble, in an odd way, because they feel that by not trying they are at least "being honest." Furthermore, they believe making no grand attempts will prevent them from doing the damage they've witnessed hypocrites doing. Theirs is a sort of laid-back spirituality. Matters of Christian engagement such as Scripture, sacrament, community, and service are optional. Just live your life.

One problem though—Jesus said, "As the Father has sent me, I am sending you" (John 20:21). Don't just sit back and play Xbox while the world destroys itself.

The second camp, on beholding the beauty of Jesus, summon a massive internal rally to try to live like him. These are the folks providing most of the army for Christian activity, the heroes held up in church, the ones fighting for justice across the globe. Bless them, they are engaged. But let me tell you, few things can mess you up as badly as trying to do your best. For the tender heart, the earnest heart, it is *so* discouraging to give all you have trying to do what you think Jesus would have you do, and find yourself falling short, sabotaging your own efforts at every turn. Discouragement and shame settle in like a long Seattle rain.

And this is what most Christians experience as the Christian life: Try harder; feel worse.

I spoke of cunning traps that replace the simple priority of loving Jesus. Here is a very surprising one—the trap of integrity. What I mean by this is when our attention turns to maintaining personal righteousness. This seems noble and right. Jesus told us to keep his commands. But this can be a trap because most Christians *interpret this* as "Try harder; do your best."

I find myself slipping back into this weekly. A handful of symptoms tip me off. Exhaustion, for one. I'll just find myself wrung out again. Or an unnamed internal distress; my insides all twisted up. Discouragement, that old nagging cloud of "I'm totally blowing it" back over me. Irritation with needy people. These symptoms—and a host of others—are the collateral damage that results from trying my best. They let me know I've fallen back to thinking that to love Jesus is to give my very best in living for him. And this is a sticky business. Because on the one hand, that's true—to love him is to obey. But out of what resources? From what fountain of inner strength?

I thought it was my faithfulness. My integrity. A willingness to sacrifice, to fight well. And of course we are involved; of course our choices matter. But didn't Jesus warn, "Apart from me you can do nothing" (John 15:5)? The good news is this—you were never meant to imitate Christ. Not if by that you mean doing your best to live as he did. It ought to come as a great relief. Something inside me says, *Well—that's certainly been my experience.* But without understanding that I was *never meant to do my best,* I feel awful about it.

In a biography of Christ which is good in many aspects, I ran across this terrible snare. The author describes the mission of Jesus as,

> a spiritual revolution, the replacement of the unreformed law of Moses by a New Testament based on love and neighborliness, which could be embraced by all classes and all peoples. . . . Life on earth was to be devoted to a self-transformation in which each human soul strove to become as like God as possible, a process made easier by the existence of his son made man, thus facilitating imitation.

It is an evil and crippling distortion. Jesus didn't start the Peace Corps. The secret of Christianity is something else altogether—the life of Christ in you. Allowing his life to become your life. His revolution is not self-transformation, but *his* transformation of us, from the inside out, as we receive his life and allow him to live through us. Vine, branch. Anything else is madness.

"But there is a reality in which all things are easy and plain," Mac-Donald promises,

> Oneness, that is, with the Lord of Life. . . . As Christ is the blossom of humanity, so the blossom of every man is the Christ perfected in him. The vital force of humanity working in him is Christ; he is his root—the generator and perfecter of his individuality. The stronger the pure will of the man to be true, the freer and more active his choice, the more definite his individuality, ever the more is the man and all that is his, Christ's.[3]

The blossom of your humanity is the life of Jesus in you. You get to live his life! Or what is salvation after all?

God knew what he was doing from the very beginning. He decided from the outset to shape the lives of those who love him along the same lines as the life of his Son. The Son stands first in the line of humanity he restored. We see the original and intended shape of our lives there in him. After God made that decision of what his children should be like, he followed it up by calling people by name. After he called them by name, he set them on a solid basis with himself. And then, after getting them established, he stayed with them to the end, gloriously completing what he had begun. (ROMANS 8:29–30 The Message)

Jesus stands first in the line of humanity that God is restoring. He is not merely a model—that would be unreachable, crushing. He is the *means* by which God is restoring our humanity. That is what Christianity is supposed to do to a person. This happens as his life invades ours.

But the idea of redemption as the *impartation of a life* provides a totally different framework of understanding. God's seminal redemptive act toward us is the communication of a new kind of life, as the seed—one of our Lord's most favored symbols— carries a new life into the enfolding soil. Turning from old ways with faith and hope in Christ stands forth as the natural first expression of the new life imparted. That life will be poised to become a life of the same quality as Christ's, because it indeed *is* Christ's. He really does live on in us. The incarnation continues.[4]

The incarnation continues...in you.

But How?

Love Jesus. Let him be himself with you. Allow his life to fill yours.

Every day, give him your life to be filled with his. This is part of what I now pray, every morning:

Lord Jesus, I give my life to you today, to live your life.

Of course, this assumes that you are willing to surrender your self-determination. You'll find it hard to receive his life in any great measure if you as the branch keep running off on your own, leaving the Vine behind in order to do life as you please. Honestly, I think this is why we accept such a bland Jesus, or a distant Jesus—he doesn't intrude on our plans. I said earlier that one of the most bizarre realities of the religious church is how loving Jesus is considered optional, extra credit. The same sort of madness has crept in with the idea that you can be a Christian and hold on to your self-determination.

And how is that going, by the way?

If you are not drawing your life from Jesus, it means you are trying to draw it from some other source. I'll guarantee you that it's not working.

Jesus was simply stating a fact of nature when he said, "Whoever wants to save his life will lose it, but whoever loses his life for me will find it" (Matt. 16:25). Grab for life and it falls through your fingers like sand; give your life away to God, and you will be a person his life can fill. If you want the real deal, if you want to experience the lush, generous, unquenchable, unstoppable life of Jesus in you and through you, then surrender your self-determination.

Lord Jesus, I give my life to you today, to live your life.

The more you give the parts of your life over to Jesus, the more his life is able to invade yours. The relief alone is worth the price.

Last night Stasi and I were at a dinner party with friends we love and enjoy. It was one of those occasions where, for some reason, my internal world was not in sync with the external. All night long I was constantly aware of awful things inside me—wanting to be the center of attention, getting irritated at people for their idiosyncrasies, pride puffing up when someone told a story of personal failure—just a nightmare of sin. This morning when I woke the temptation was like New Year's Day—rushing to make all sorts of resolutions to be a better person. As I sat down to pray, I felt myself resolving to do this and that, despising this and that about me—basically, trying to kill the unattractive parts and buttress myself to be good.

It was a train wreck waiting to happen.

The Achilles' heel of this sort of "repentance" is that it is all still based in self effort. Thank God I saw it, and turned to Christ in me—asked Jesus to come and have my life more deeply. The relief was almost immediate. Not in the sense that all those flaws went poof like in a fairy tale, but rather that first, I was rescued from days and weeks of striving and self-resolve. Second, that the presence of Jesus in me does make those flaws recede into the background—some crucified, others to receive his healing grace. But the point being, this time I was able to turn to *Christ in me* as my only hope of transformation, and the fruit of this turning-to is profound relief.

So, I am giving my life over to Jesus to live his life every day, and, as I move through my day and encounter this or that test, what I now pray—when I remember to—is this:

Jesus in me, help me with this.

We call upon Christ *in us* to help us in the moment. For as the once-tormented Augustine discovered, Jesus is "more interior" to each of us "than we are to ourselves."[5]

By the way, this is the point of encountering those things in your life you cannot handle—you are forced to turn to Christ. Did you really think you could be kind for the rest of your life without the inner help of Jesus? One day of kindness is a miracle. What about forgiving? Generous? Honest? Did you really think you could overcome your lifelong strongholds without some sort of Lazarus-like breakthrough? It simply isn't going to happen—not without the life of Jesus in you.

This realization was an epiphany for me.

I have spent most of my adult years trying to find those keys that would enable people to become whole. Like an archaeologist raking for buried treasure, I've combed through the provinces of counseling, spiritual discipline, inner healing, deliverance, addiction recovery—anything that would help me help others get better. Like Schliemann when his shovel struck the buried ruins of Troy, the epiphany I have come to is this:

Jesus has no intention of letting you become whole apart from his moment-to-moment presence and life within you.

Your brokenness and your sin are not something you overcome *so that* you can walk with God. They are the occasions for you to cry out for the life of God in you to rescue you. Not God outside you, up in the sky somewhere. Christ *in* you, your only hope of glory. Let this sink in: Jesus has no intention of letting you become whole apart from his moment-to-moment presence and life within you.

If you have found forgiveness in Christ, thank God. But you are still a branch in desperate need of a Vine. If you have found his morality, wonderful. But you can't hope to pull it off without his life. If you have found inspiration in Christ, rejoice. But it will last two days without his life. "Our only task," said Oswald Chambers, "is to maintain a vital connection with Jesus Christ, seeing that nothing interferes with it."[6]

This was the point of the Vine-branch metaphor. The same moment Jesus gave us that, he urged us to "remain" in him:

> Remain in me, and I will remain in you. No branch can bear fruit by itself; it must remain in the vine. Neither can you bear fruit unless you remain in me. I am the vine; you are the branches. If a man remains in me and I in him, he will bear much fruit; apart from me you can do nothing. (JOHN 15:4–5)

How do we remain in vital union with him? By loving him, by obeying him, by surrendering more and more and more of ourselves to him. This is how Jesus lived, by the way. He modeled for us a totally surrendered life, a life lived in union with the Father: "I tell you the truth, the Son can do nothing by himself; he can do only what he sees his Father doing. . . . For I did not speak of my own accord, but the Father who sent me commanded me what to say and how to say it" (John 5:19; 12:49). He came in part to show us how it's done. All that dynamic life you see coursing through him, he received it as we must do—through ongoing love and dependence upon God.

Now, we must give our lives over to him in order to receive his life. Not just once, but as a regular practice. Of course there is more to this than saying a prayer. It would take another book to describe the ways we make ourselves available to his life. We find those practices that help us receive the life of God. Whether it be prayer, worship, silence, sacrament, or the gift of sunshine, sitting beside a stream, music, adventure—we seek out those things that help us to receive the life of God. You have a personal guide now; ask Jesus what to take up and what to set down, so that you might receive his life.

By the way, this is the bottom-line test of anything claiming to be of Jesus: Does it bring *life*? If it doesn't, drop it like a rattlesnake. And you will find that the religious never, ever brings life. Ever. That is its greatest exposure.

This Alone Will Change the World

One of the reasons we like our friends is because we like who we are when we are with them. Wow, is this true of Jesus—when he and I are close, I like who I am. When we seem to be distant, I am a disaster. Well dressed, perhaps, putting a good face on things, but lifeless—like a cut flower. As a buddy said over lunch the other day, "When I'm in Christ or he's in me or however you describe that, everything is different—the way I see myself, the way I see you. I am the man I want to be."

As we love him, experience him, allow his life to fill ours, the personality of Jesus transforms our personalities. The timid become bold and the bold become patient and the patient become fierce and the uptight become free and the religious become scandalously good. "They looked to Him and were radiant" (Psalm 34:5 NASB). They looked to Jesus and became like him. Loving Jesus helps us to become what human beings were meant to be. As Athanasius said, "He became what we are that we might become what he is."

We aren't the only ones who need this desperately; the world needs this to happen in us.

You realize that—whether we know it or not, whether we like it or not—in all our efforts we are continually portraying the personality of God to the world. A sobering thought. Take an evening and cruise the Internet; see what Christianity looks like to the world. It will make you mighty angry; at least, it better. No wonder the world turns away. At least God still has nature speaking on his behalf.

What enormous good would it do in the world if churches were known as playful, witty, fierce, humble, generous, honest, cunning, beautiful, and true? When we hold fast to a bland Jesus, we get a bland church. A two-dimensional Jesus equals two-dimensional Christians. As Swinburne lamented,

> Thou hast conquered, O pale Galilean;
> the world has grown grey from thy breath.[7]

That is the tragic effect of the religious Jesus and the religious church upon the world.

But *this* Jesus—this Beautiful Outlaw—if his exquisite life were to invade ours...oh, my. It would change everything.

Jesus, invade my life. Cleanse this temple. Produce your Cana in me. I give my humanity to you, to be restored by your humanity. I give my life to you to live your life.

Then the incarnation *can* continue.

ONE LAST THOUGHT

And now I must confess: I am a bit anxious.

Soon you will set this book down, and I am desperately searching for the right words to say, like a mother and father standing on the railway platform seeing their son off to war. I am groping for the words that will somehow move you to *hold on to this*. The train blows its whistle; the mother chokes up and the father clasps the last handshake ever so tightly, because they know what is at stake. My friends, so much is at stake.

Two things must be said; I will hold myself to two.

They are found late in the book of Hebrews, late in the Bible. They seem to be spoken in the same spirit of a railway platform farewell:

Let us fix our eyes on Jesus, the author and perfecter of our faith, who for the joy set before him endured the cross, scorning its shame, and sat down at the right hand of the throne of God. Consider him who endured such opposition from sinful men, so that you will not grow weary and lose heart. (12:2–3)

"I do not want you to lose heart," the author says in a fatherly way, his hand reluctant to let ours go. "Fix your gaze on Jesus." The context of the passage is suffering, hardship, and opposition. We are urged to cling to Jesus. So, I must say something about suffering, and clinging. An honest book about Jesus that does not address suffering is not an honest book.

Surely you have noticed that we have entered a time of great suffering on the earth. More than a million children are prostituted into the sex trade each year, forced into daily sexual encounters with adults that leave their psyches shattered. One is heinous; ten an atrocity; hundreds of thousands and I cannot even speak. On a recent trip to Africa, a friend saw young girls lying on sidewalks at night, covered only with a blanket, offering themselves for thirty cents.

There are 143,000,000 orphans in the world today. Thirty-five million people worldwide have HIV. Twenty-seven million souls are currently slaves—more than any other time on earth. Then there are the wars, earthquakes, famines. I need not go on; you watch the news. And Jesus warned us about this. Before his death, his teaching turned very sober—nothing that would make a best seller in this world of "tell me how to make life work *now*."

You will hear of wars and threats of wars, but don't panic. Yes, these things must take place, but the end won't follow immediately. Nation will go to war against nation, and kingdom against kingdom. There will be famines and earthquakes in many parts of the world. But all this is only the first of the birth

pains, with more to come. Then you will be arrested, persecuted, and killed. You will be hated all over the world because
you are my followers. And many will turn away from me and
betray and hate each other. And many false prophets will appear
and will deceive many people. Sin will be rampant everywhere,
and the love of many will grow cold. But the one who endures
to the end will be saved.... See, I have warned you. (MATTHEW
24:4–13, 25 NLT)

Well...the man certainly knew how to shoot straight. If such as
this was coming, the only loving thing to do was to cry out a warning.
I'll not be making apocalyptic predictions, but I do want to point this
out: Suffering is flooding the earth like a rising tide. This isn't merely
something we behold on the news. In the past six months nearly
everyone dear to me has passed through a dark valley of suffering; so
has our family. I'll bet if you think of ten people you know, six are in
the midst of some painful ordeal even now.

When a close friend called me from the hospital, I knew it was
bad. There were tears, and a desperate plea for prayer. His younger
brother—newly married—was headed into a sudden, dangerous
surgery for an aggressive brain tumor. The prognosis was very grim.
His family was reeling; urgent prayers were being sent up by many. I
knew that a season of suffering was coming for everyone involved:
anguish, confusion, and all the terrible dangers that follow hard on
the heels of pain. When one life is hurting, the suffering reverberates
out through many lives, multiplying, compounding; this is the story
the statistics never tell.

Listen carefully (this is the father on the platform, fumbling for
those last words): Suffering will try to separate you from Jesus. You
must not let it.

The worst part of suffering is the damage it can do to your view of God, your relationship with him. Feelings of abandonment creep in: *Why did he let this happen?* Anger. A loss of hope. Mistrust. Forsakenness. At the very time you need him most, you will feel most compelled to pull away from Jesus, or feel that he has pulled away from you. This is what the father who wrote Hebrews was trying to prevent.

There is a popular theology out there that says a Christian can avoid suffering. (You can understand why it's popular. Most of us have embraced it without even knowing—simply notice your reaction when life turns on you.) It is a devastating heresy because suffering will come, and then what will you do? The ground heaves beneath you, shaking your faith in God because you thought it wouldn't come, shouldn't come. It gets you scrambling; it can level you for a long time if you thought you'd escape it.

Be very, very careful and pay attention to how you *interpret* your suffering. Don't jump to conclusions. Interpretation is critical. Beware the agreements that you make. This is where the enemy can destroy you. Agreements such as *God has abandoned me; it's my fault; I've done something wrong,* and a host of others. If you've been making these agreements, you will want to break them. They allow a chasm to form between you and your Jesus.

By all means, seek a breakthrough. Too many Christians simply fold under hardship and give way to the feelings of abandonment. Pray against it; pray hard. If it is an attack from the enemy, much of that can be shut down through prayer. Much healing is available, too, through the life of Jesus in us. Do not simply surrender. But when breakthrough does not seem to come, when the pain lingers on, remember this:

Just as the sufferings of Christ flow over into our lives, so also through Christ our comfort overflows. (2 CORINTHIANS 1:5)

Your suffering is neither pointless nor isolated. Somehow, Jesus' sufferings overflow into our lives; somehow ours are linked to his. This is a great honor. It grants our sorrows an incredible dignity; it invites us to know an intimacy and connection with Jesus in them, *because* of them. The sufferings of Jesus are the noblest part of his life story; the cross, the crown of thorns. What an unspeakable honor that he would share even this with us. This fellowship is a treasure we have not tapped into but one we will need.

When his suffering overflows into our lives, God's promise is that his comfort will overflow to us as well. We can cry out for the comfort of God. Whatever your circumstances may be, he *will* heal your wounded heart; he *will* comfort. Cling to him. "My soul clings to you; your right hand upholds me" (Ps. 63:8). He is with you now. For his name is Faithful and True.

So this is what Hebrews is trying to say: Do not lose heart because of your suffering; cling to Jesus.

Do whatever it takes to help you fix your gaze back upon this Beautiful Outlaw. "I say his name every time I take the stairs in our house," my friend Becky told me. "As I go up or down, each step I say the name 'Jesus.'"

"How many times is that?" I asked.

She chuckled. "Oh...lots. Twenty times up or down those stairs a day. It brings me back to him."

That's the idea—find those things that help you remember Jesus, turn your heart toward him throughout the day. As you do, his presence becomes more real; his love can come to you, and his life can fill you.

I try to keep a CD of favorite worship music in my car. I have a collection of odd items on my desk—several rocks, a piece of driftwood, a few hawk feathers, a seashell, an arrowhead. They are reminders, icons of God's coming to me. Coming for me. *Coming through for me.* I need all the help I can get. I have notes, Scriptures, words from Jesus taped around my office, even on my bathroom mirror. Now I write them on my hand. Whatever it takes.

The enemy would love nothing more than for you to set this book down, walk away, and forget. If you read this in one sitting, you just drove ninety through Prague. It's safe to say you missed a bit. Go back; soak it in a second time. Read back over these stories and examples of his personality, and as you do, tell him you love him: "I love this about you, Jesus. Show me this in my life; be yourself with me." And as you behold him in these pages, say to yourself, *I get to live like this. This is the Jesus who now lives in me; this life is inside me.*

Last night during a gathering here in our home, I was filmed reading passages of this book to a handful of friends. I think those videos will help you experience Jesus even more deeply. You can find them at www.beautifuloutlaw.net.

"Without a friend thou canst not live long," said Thomas à Kempis, "and if Jesus be not thy friend, above all thou shalt be sad and desolate." We may not recognize our desolation for what it really is—a longing for Jesus. We might mistake it for disappointment with friends or spouse, for restlessness or loneliness or even depression. The human soul was made for friendship with Jesus, and if we have not that...well, it won't matter what we have. So cling to him; fix your eyes on him.

"What are you looking forward to with Jesus?"

It was the close of an interview. Almost as an afterthought, the interviewer tossed in this final question. Honestly, it threw me. For a long pause, a rather embarrassingly long pause, the kind you can drive a truck through, I didn't know what to say. My heart was racing to catch up with the reality the question assumed. *What am I looking forward to with Jesus?* I was sideswiped by how little I ever thought about it. That was the embarrassing part. Though I love Jesus dearly, I hadn't been thinking about our future together; I'd been lost in trying to make life work. (And then the suffering just made me mad and disheartened.) Like a cold plunge, the question shocked me awake to the fact that I *do* believe I will see Jesus face-to-face. One day soon; sooner than later. Then my heart began to rise past embarrassment toward an incredible hope: I'm not only going to see Jesus, I'm going to share life with him!

Toward the end of his days on earth, as the darkness of Maundy Thursday and Good Friday raced toward him, Jesus gave us this remarkable promise:

> In the re-creation of the world, when the Son of Man will rule gloriously, you who have followed me will also rule, starting with the twelve tribes of Israel. And not only you, but anyone who sacrifices home, family, fields—whatever—because of me will get it all back a hundred times over, not to mention the considerable bonus of eternal life. (MATTHEW 19:28–29 The Message)

Did you catch that? *The re-creation of the world*! The religious fog would have us believe that when we die we go to church forever, there to sing hymns for millennia. A horrible distortion, and *not* the future as Jesus understood it. He called the next chapter "the re-creation of the world," sometimes translated as "the renewal of all things" (NIV, NRSV). A renewed heavens, a renewed earth. My friends, I hope you understand that we get the entire glorious kingdom back. Sunlight on water; songbirds in a forest; desert sands under moonlight; vineyards just before harvest—Jesus fully intends to restore the glorious world he gave us. Paradise lost; paradise regained. A hundred times over.

This was what was in his own thoughts when he said, as he passed the cup to his brothers in the upper room just hours before Gethsemane and the Gestapo, "I'll not be drinking wine from this cup again until that new day when I'll drink with you in the kingdom of my Father" (Matt. 26:29 The Message). Jesus knew as sure as he knew anything that a new day was coming and with it a glorious kingdom. And there he knew we would feast again—not merely sing—and raise our glasses, and he would break his fast. Food, drink, laughter, life. The joy set before him. Cana was just a foretaste.

Reading this verse, my son Blaine empathized to Jesus, *You've been waiting a long time for that glass of wine.* In his wry, honest, playful way, Jesus replied, *Tell me about it.*

Back to the interview. Finally, I answered: "Spearfishing." I know this beautiful world will be ours again and so will Jesus, and all the time imaginable to play together. Beauty. Intimacy. Adventure. The very things we were given at the dawn of time. But honestly, more than all that, I'm just looking forward to seeing him, looking into his eyes, hugging him as Peter did on the beach and not letting go for a very long time.

So I pass the question to you: What are you looking forward to with Jesus? It will do your heart good to let your hopes run in his direction.

Meanwhile, make a practice of loving Jesus. Let him be himself with you. Let his life fill yours. Oh, and one more thing (the train begins to pull away). Do you recall from chapter 14 what Jesus said to Kylie as they reached the top of the mountain together? She saw a gathering of people milling around, and Jesus said, "Introduce me."

It's one of the ways we love him—we introduce others to him. If you've found this book helpful, tell your friends! There are a lot of folks out there who desperately need to know this Beautiful Outlaw.

Until the second Cana.

ACKNOWLEDGMENTS

My sincerest thanks to Rielynn Simons for her research; to Rolf Zettersten, Joey Paul, and the team at FaithWords; and to Sealy and Curtis Yates. My eternal love as well to all those who have helped me know this Jesus, this Beautiful Outlaw.

NOTES

CHAPTER 1: THE PLAYFULNESS OF GOD AND THE POISON OF RELIGION

1. David J. Duncan, *The River Why* (San Francisco: Sierra Club Books, 1983), 14–15, italics in original.
2. George MacDonald, *Unspoken Sermons: Series I, II, and III* (Charleston, SC: BiblioBazaar, 2006), 261.

CHAPTER 3: IS JESUS REALLY *PLAYFUL*?

1. Frederick Buechner, *Telling the Truth: The Gospel as Tragedy, Comedy, and Fairy Tale* (New York: HarperCollins, 1977), 49–50.

CHAPTER 4: FIERCE INTENTION

1. C. S. Lewis, *Perelandra* (New York: Scribner, 1972), 12.
2. Ibid.
3. Ibid., 13–14, italics in original.
4. G. K. Chesterton, *The Everlasting Man* (Radford, VA: Wilder, 2008), 118.
5. Ibid., 131, 132.

CHAPTER 5: THE MOST HUMAN FACE OF ALL

1. Brennan Manning, *Abba's Child: The Cry of the Heart for Intimate Belonging* (Colorado Springs: NavPress, 2002), 89.

2. G. K. Chesterton, *The Everlasting Man* (Radford, VA: Wilder, 2008), 116.

3. Eugene H. Peterson, *Christ Plays in Ten Thousand Places: A Conversation in Spiritual Theology* (Grand Rapids: Eerdmans, 2005), 35, 59.

CHAPTER 6: EXTRAVAGANT GENEROSITY

1. Bonaventure, *The Soul's Journey into God*, ed. Ewert H. Cousins (Mahwah, NJ: Paulist Press, 1978), 30, 69.

CHAPTER 7: DISRUPTIVE HONESTY

1. M. Scott Peck, *The Road Less Traveled* (New York: Simon & Schuster, 2003), 50.

CHAPTER 8: A SCANDALOUS FREEDOM

1. Paul Johnson, *Jesus: A Biography from a Believer* (New York: Viking, 2010), 109.

2. Dorothy Sayer. Specific source unknown.

CHAPTER 11: TRUENESS

1. C. S. Lewis, *The Horse and His Boy*, The Chronicles of Narnia, bk. 3 (New York: HarperCollins, 1982), 175–77.

CHAPTER 13: LOVING JESUS

1. G. K. Chesterton, *St. Francis of Assisi* (New York: Random House, 2001), 7, 8.

CHAPTER 15: CLEARING AWAY
THE RELIGIOUS FOG

1. Eugene H. Peterson, *Christ Plays in Ten Thousand Places: A Conversation in Spiritual Theology* (Grand Rapids: Eerdmans, 2005), 34–35.

2. Edna St. Vincent Millay, "To Jesus on His Birthday," in A. Bonner, ed., *Poetry Society of America Anthology* (New York: Fine Editions, 1946), 151–52.

CHAPTER 16: LETTING JESUS BE HIMSELF—ENCOUNTERS

1. Augustine, *Confessions*, trans. R. S. Pine-Coffin (New York: Penguin, 1961), 177.
2. Joseph Mary Plunkett, "I See His Blood upon the Rose," in *Poems* (Ithaca, NY: Cornell University Library, 2009), 50.

CHAPTER 17: LETTING HIS LIFE FILL YOURS

1. See www.borealforest.org.
2. George MacDonald, *Unspoken Sermons: Series I, II, and III* (Charleston, SC: BiblioBazaar, 2006), 209.
3. Ibid., 158, 320–21.
4. Dallas Willard, *The Spirit of the Disciplines: Understanding How God Changes Lives* (New York: HarperCollins, 1988), 38, italics in original.
5. Augustine, *Confessions*, 111, 6, trans. R. S. Pine-Coffin (New York: Penguin, 1961).
6. Oswald Chambers, *My Utmost for His Highest* (Grand Rapids: Discover House, 1992), March 25.
7. Algernon C. Swinburne, "Hymn to Proserpine," in *Poems and Ballads and Atalanta in Calydon*, ed. Kenneth Haynes (New York: Penguin, 2000), 57.

I WANT MORE OF THIS JESUS!

I WANT TO SHARE HIM WITH OTHERS!

WWW.BeautifulOutlaw.net

Beautiful Outlaw Videos for Streaming and Downloading

Beautiful Outlaw Book Trailer (send it to friends!)

Beautiful Outlaw Study Guide Download

Live Outlaw events and webcasts!

Share your stories of how Jesus is coming for you

COME BE A PART OF THE

MOST BEAUTIFUL REVOLUTION EVER!

LIVE TEACHINGS
from JOHN ELDREDGE

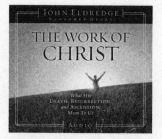

The Work of Christ
What His Death, Resurrection, and Ascension Mean to Us

If we were to pick one word to describe God's will for your life, that word would be *Restoration*.

There's far more to the work of Jesus than just forgiveness through the Cross. While the Cross is central, many people have missed out on the power of the Resurrection and the Ascension – the power of restoration and healing, the power to live as we were meant to live.

Discover the power to restore you—as a woman or a man whose life is filled with the radiance of God.

The Good Heart

Is your heart good or bad? Can you trust that God will speak to you in your heart? That your desires can be from God? Scripture teaches that the heart is central to our lives. Yet, many Christians find it hard to even talk about matters of the heart. God's transformation of our hearts has far-reaching implications – for our relationships, our calling, and our walk with God. The truth will set you free. Truly.

The Hope of Prayer – *Things Can Be Different*

Every one of us can point to things in our lives that we'd like to see change. And to help us bring about that change, God has given us prayer. The Scriptures talk a lot about prayer, but we're not really sure what to do with it, or, more importantly, *how* to do it. In this series, John Eldredge shows us how to pray with hope and confidence and how to apply prayer to our lives. There are few thoughts as hopeful as the thought that things *can* be different. And so the disciples said, "Teach us to pray."

Find these and many, many more – only available at
WWW.RANSOMEDHEART.COM

REVISED *and* EXPANDED
EDITIONS

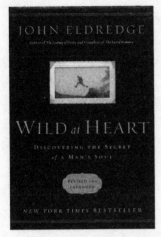

Wild at Heart

Every man was once a boy. And every little boy has dreams, big dreams: dreams of being the hero, of beating the bad guys, doing daring feats and rescuing the damsel in distress. But what happens to those dreams when they grow up? In *Wild at Heart*, John Eldredge invites men to recover their masculine heart, defined in the image of a passionate God. And he invites women to discover the secret of a man's soul and to delight in the strength and wildness men were created to offer.

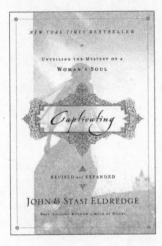

Captivating

Every woman was once a little girl. And every little girl holds in her heart her most precious dreams. She longs to be swept up into a romance, to play an irreplaceable role in a great adventure, to *be* the beauty of the story. Those desires are far more than child's play. They are the secret to the feminine heart.

The message of *Captivating* is this: Your heart matters more than anything else in all creation. The desires you had as a little girl and the longings you still feel as a woman are telling you of the life God created you to live. He offers to come now as the Hero of your story, to rescue your heart and release you to live as a fully alive and feminine woman. A woman who is truly captivating.

Expanded and Revised editions give John and Stasi the chance to write new introductions, address some issues in the book that confused folks, and offer new epilogues and additional prayers for transformation.

Available wherever books are sold.